THIS QUEER ARAB FAMILY

Elias Jahshan (he/him) is a Palestinian Lebanese journalist and writer. He is the editor of *This Arab Is Queer: An Anthology by LGBTQ+ Arab Writers* (Saqi, 2022), which was a finalist for the Lambda Literary Awards and shortlisted for the Bread & Roses Award. His writing has been published in collections including *Arab, Australian, Other: Stories on Race and Identity* (ed. Randa Abdel-Fattah & Sara Saleh; Picador, 2019) and *Ask the Night for a Dream: Palestinian Writing From the Diaspora* (ed. Susan Muaddi Darraj; Palestine Writes Press, 2024). Elias is a former editor of *Star Observer*, Australia's longest-running queer media outlet. He has written for *The Guardian*, *Gay Times*, *Attitude*, *The New Arab* and *My Kali*, among others. Born and raised in Sydney, he lives in London.

THIS QUEER ARAB FAMILY

An Anthology by LGBTQ+ Arab Writers

Edited by Elias Jahshan

SAQI

SAQI BOOKS
Gable House, 18-24 Turnham Green Terrace
London W4 1QP
www.saqibooks.com

First published by Saqi Books 2025

ISBN 978 1 84925 088 7
eISBN 978 1 84925 089 4

A full CIP record for this book is available from the British Library.

The EU GPSR authorised representative is Logos Europe,
9 rue Nicolas Poussin, 17000 La Rochelle, France.
Email: contact@logoseurope.eu

Printed and bound by Clays Ltd, Elcograf S.p.A

CONTENTS

ELIAS JAHSHAN

INTRODUCTION

Family is everything in Arab cultures. Our families are known to be loud, large and loving. Yes, we're also nosey and in everyone's business, but that's because our familial bonds run deep. Arab hospitality is legendary – the desire to feed our friends and loved ones is built into our DNA. Entering our homes is like stepping into a warm embrace.

When I think of family, I think of the Arabic word *hafla*. *Hafla* means 'party', but it can also mean the act of caring for others. It's a fitting word to describe this collection, where ten queer Arab writers share what family and community means to them. These complex, nuanced and real-life stories go beyond the self. Some challenge outdated patriarchal norms, while others find ways to honour traditions that are worth preserving. Here, readers learn how queer Arabs forge kinships and celebrate culture on their own terms and hold space for one another through activism and community solidarity, navigating their place within their existing families or building their own. Together, these narratives embrace the many ways LGBTQ+ Arabs find – and keep close – relatives and the friends we choose to become our families, in the Arab world and in the diaspora, today.

Each of the writers presented here skilfully articulates

how they move through family dynamics as queer Arabs with honesty and integrity. They are forging new ways, while remembering old ones. Each piece is raw and reflective, both deeply personal and universal. They acknowledge the realities we face, while also offering hope for what the future has in store for us. Their stories range widely from one another and come together as a perfect whole.

There is no better way to introduce you to the collection than through offering a brief insight into each of the pieces, so you can see for yourself the broad, extraordinary range of writing to come. Shrouk El-Attar begins 'Dancing Queer' at home, during a horrific night raid by British immigration authorities that ripped her family apart. With rich, compelling storytelling, she describes how she channels the trauma of such a harrowing experience by raising money and attention for immigrant and educational causes. After navigating huge obstacles both personally and professionally, Shrouk combines her bearded, belly dancing alter ego and impressive engineering career with the creation of a non-binary dancing robot, which she uses to teach and inspire future scientists.

Technology has a huge impact on how we live and love today. In 'One Way Trip to The Moon: My Journey With OnlyFans' Zeid Al-Nasr details his departure from Syria during the civil war to Canada, by way of South Africa. The way Zeid recounts his story, brimming with resilience and kindness, is humbling. In Canada, he was able to pay for higher education and create a parasocial community through online sex work. This in turn allowed him to go from the estranged son to the son who provides and ensures his family is looked after, albeit from afar.

All families look different. Though we're led to believe that family is everything, as queer Arabs, we don't see ourselves reflected in a heteronormative structure, where communal bonds are revered and personal desires are subsumed in favour of family unity. In 'My Brown Girl', Nahid Toubia takes readers on a journey to Sudan, by way of Egypt, as she spends weeks looking for the baby who would become her daughter. Told with heart and warmth, Nahid offers readers an honest portrayal of what she had to go through to adopt several decades ago.

While Nahid's path to adoption began in the 1990s, husbands Karim Chedid and Andrew Delatolla are, at the time of writing, still at the early stages of their adoption process. In 'A Family of Our Own', they write eloquently about wanting to start a family of their own. In looking to their future, they discover that the process of adoption has also given them pause to reflect on their family history.

From adoption to the maternity ward, in 'To You, Child of Our Resistance and Our Joys' Lamiae Bouqentar writes a letter to Sosoa, the newborn baby of her life partner and best friend who's also her ex. The letter offers an emergent form of worldmaking in which Arab queer life, resistance, visibility, opacity, love, care and joy are re-envisioned beyond state recognition or the nuclear family. Tender and touching, 'To You, Child of Our Resistance and Our Joys' looks forward to sharing Arab heritage with the next generation.

But just as new life enters the world, so too do we have

to learn how to let go. In 'From a Windowless Room in Mecca', Melhem Hasan writes about his Hajj pilgrimage with his parents, shortly before his father's death. This piece is not only about religious validation, but also about emotional claustrophobia, queerness in sacred spaces and the struggle for connection – divine or familial – in moments of profound loss. In the absence of light and space, Melhem writes with startling clarity about how he drew strength in the darkest of moments from unexpected places and all the while remembering to breathe.

Sinin Nakhle's essay 'Who Is It That You Love?' also considers our physicality. Through memory beats and narrative snapshots, Sinin remembers the care his grandparents had for one another's bodies in their old age. Sinin too is aware of his body, sharing his transition journey as he navigates medical gatekeeping and touch as a love language. From Lebanon to Europe, the body becomes the site of care, belonging and becoming.

The body also becomes a tool for safety. In 'Learning From Other Mothers at a Time of Genocide', Randa Jarrar shares how she raised 20,000 US dollars, strapped it to her body, flew to Cairo and distributed the money to Palestinians who were fleeing the genocide in Gaza. In Cairo, after meeting Palestinian mothers, she discovers a new, bittersweet appreciation for motherhood and for her queer comrades.

From activism to Australia, in 'Club Arak: Twenty-three Years of Partying, Politics and Protest' the club night's co-founder, Alissar Gazal, reflects on the longest-running queer Arab club night outside the Southwest Asia and North Africa

(SWANA) region: Club Arak, in my hometown, Sydney. Thanks to Club Arak, I was able to explore the joy of being gay and Arab at the same time. Club Arak and the friends I made through it gave me the courage to be my authentic self with my family, overcoming the shame that riddled my teens and early twenties. Two decades later, I am still friends with some of the people I met, laughed and danced with during those years. I am thrilled that Alissar used this space to consider how politics and partying played a role in fostering a much-needed safe space and community for Sydney's queer Arab community.

Alongside those who share their decades of wisdom, it is a privilege to include some writers who are at a relatively early stage in their career. 'My Mother's Pronouns' by Abu Leila looks at the ways that migrants build families with other displaced people. Here, Abu Leila uses stark prose, direct speech and open conversation to convey a short memoir, told in vignettes, with dark humour and light touch. Readers get a glimpse of the sisterhood and fierce matriarchal protection that helped form who Abu Leila is today.

Editing each of these chapters has given me pause to reflect on what the future holds for queer Arab storytelling. I can honestly say it looks promising.

Half the writers featured in *This Queer Arab Family* were invited to share their stories, while the other half were selected from a public open call for submissions. I was blown away by the response to the open call: ninety-two submissions were made from all corners of the world, including Casablanca, Riyadh, Beirut, Dubai, Amman, Baghdad, Jerusalem and Ramallah;

Athens, London, Paris, Berlin, Belfast, Barcelona, Glasgow, Venice and Amsterdam; New York, Toronto, Los Angeles, Sydney, Melbourne, San Francisco, Ohio, Vancouver, Miami, Panama and beyond. Some pieces were written in Arabic and French, as well as in English. It was a joy and privilege to read each one. It is worth reflecting on some of the findings from this large body of queer Arab writing, so that you can see the vibrant places LGBTQ+ Arabs are exploring.

The geographies of the writers who responded to the open call represent the full range of nationalities from across the Levant, Gulf, North Africa and Mesopotamian regions, and are a mix of those living in the Arab world or as part of the immigrant diaspora. The diaspora experiences also range hugely, from those born and raised in the Arab world to the children or grandchildren of immigrants. Some writers straddle the middle ground, splitting their time equally between the diaspora and the SWANA region, where their families still reside. There are also several writers who cannot return home, either due to safety reasons or because they are Palestinian and are denied the right of return.

The diversity in locations of the writers and their experiences proves that there is no one right way to be Arab or queer, and indeed that no hierarchy of such experience should exist. The submissions are written in various forms of narrative nonfiction, including essays, short memoirs, vignettes and letters. The power of place was prominent. One writer shared their experience of a hook-up gone wrong in Cairo that resulted in an arrest, which gave rise to their reflections on their profound love for the city itself. Other writers share stories on 'reverse diaspora', where they come of age and embrace their identities after moving back to Tunisia, Lebanon or Egypt.

Many used the open call as a chance to reflect on the intersection of sexuality and faith – both Muslim and Christian. A few writers argue that queer Arab kinship redefines family as a spiritual and political expression, and that this kinship transcends traditional notions of blood ties, gender or heteronormativity. Other writers explore activism, solidarity and the power of reclaiming language and culture as a means of defining family. Some pieces are centred on visceral nightlife interactions, or the power of collective mourning. Israel's genocide in Gaza and the Syrian civil war rose time and time again. So did finding validation in family history and queer legacy.

Some submissions feature popular culture, television or music references, others are deeply private and personal, recounted through transcribed WhatsApp voice notes. One non-binary writer from the Gulf region penned a reflection on an online community of fellow Khaleejis that is largely anonymous, while numerous writers talked about their experiences finding parasocial connections and validation online – one writer described how an imam on the social media platform X shared their blessing.

Many of the pieces from the open call stuck with me. One writer shared a tribute to their gay, late great uncle, speaking to him from within a closet. Another tried to unpack childhood memories from Kuwait, where two women from their extended family dressed as men. Were they a couple?

Were they trans? Seemingly, they were accepted by the community at the time. These stories are a tribute to our queer Arab ancestors and a poignant reminder that we have always been here.

It was fascinating to read how language is changing how we express our experiences. English is fortunate in that it does not grapple with gender binaries (with the exception of some nouns), while Arabic is a heavily gendered language – even second-person pronouns are masculine or feminine. Some of the French memoirs submitted in the open call use *l'écriture inclusive*. French is also a gendered language. The *l'écriture inclusive* movement reevaluates how we engage with gender in language. It is a new form of French expression, whereby masculine and feminine articles are combined, with a simple dot accent between them. The emergence of *l'écriture inclusive* means masculine no longer needs to be the default for addressing mixed groups of all or no genders, as it has been historically. It is an example of how language evolves so we do not always need to choose binaries. But, in the end, we did have to choose just ten writers for this collection.

There is immense power in collecting and circulating stories. In 2022, I edited and published *This Arab Is Queer*, which enjoyed – and continues to enjoy – worldwide success. I was fortunate to meet and speak with many queer Arabs around the world, both in person and on social media. The book opened countless doors for me and I was humbled by how positively it was received. I always felt joy when Arab community members who were not queer expressed praise and support for the book in public forums, proving we have countless allies and challenging the racist trope that our queer identity is always in conflict with our culture.

The readers whose feedback means the most are fellow queer Arabs. Both books are meant for them first and foremost, after all. I have lost count of the number of times queer Arabs have approached me in person or via private messages on social media, expressing how much the representation means to them and how much they enjoyed reading *This Arab Is Queer*. Friends and acquaintances also share stories of taking – smuggling, even – copies of the book to the SWANA region, sending messages and photos via WhatsApp and Signal to tell me how much their friends cherish it.

Following a recent panel discussion at the Common Press bookshop in East London, a few people asked me to sign their copies of *This Arab Is Queer*. As I did, I noticed a Lebanese man in his early twenties and his plus one standing to the side. After I had finished signing, he approached me, somewhat nervously, to tell me how much the book meant to him. He expressed it with such heart. He said a lot of it hit close to home, especially the chapters by writers from Lebanon, where he was born and raised. As he was telling me this, it looked like his eyes were on the cusp of welling up. I expressed my gratitude, but I regret not asking if he would like a hug.

This second book is the hug we all need. One that provides a sense of comfort and warmth amid challenging times.

For many of us, the importance of family is ingrained in our psyche from a very young age. It's not uncommon for Arabs to believe that the role we play within our families impacts whether our parents and siblings command respect from others in the community. 'Coming out' looks very different for us. Many queer Arabs fear that if their true identities are public, they could bring shame on their families. It doesn't help that most Arab countries have legal statutes that criminalise same-sex activity. Penalties range from state-sanctioned discrimination to prison sentences. In a few extreme cases, it can lead to capital punishment. This ensures the stigma, shame and bigotry around queer identities remains culturally entrenched. As a result, coming out can place our safety and wellbeing at risk or lead to excommunication from the family. For many queer Arabs, these risks are too great to bear. For others, severing ties with family is a last-resort decision.

Queer Arab communities are often spoken over, either painted as passive victims of a barbaric culture in need of rescuing, or supposedly 'brainwashed' by the west. We are expected to play the role of the 'perfect victim' and deviations from this can be used to discredit us. We are stripped of our ability to share our stories on our own terms from two directions.

In recent years, we have witnessed more developments across Southwest Asia and North Africa that prove the fight for queer liberation and equality is far from over. Items emblazoned with the rainbow colours have been banned in several Gulf states and the Iraqi Parliament reinstated the criminalisation of homosexuality with jail terms of up to fifteen years. A string of political figures in Lebanon vilified the queer community in early-to-mid-2023 to distract from their own corruption and complicity in the country's devastating economic crisis, which climaxed when a group of Christian fundamentalists terrorised a bar in Beirut while it was hosting a drag show.

In the West, queer Arab bodies have been weaponised to justify and further the imperialist ambitions of nation states. This was evident amid Israel's genocidal war on the Gaza Strip, where Israeli forces and their Zionist supporters worldwide used pinkwashing (among other things) to justify the brutal military campaign. The image of an Israeli soldier, standing among the rubble and destruction of Gaza, holding up a pride flag with 'in the name of love' written on it, went viral in November 2023. This kind of propaganda is extremely damaging for queer Palestinians, among others.

These blatantly homophobic incidents or harmful pinkwashing tropes have provoked anger, and rightly so. However, the community has harnessed this anger to build and foster meaningful connections. It has proven how strong we are, why our ingenuity cannot be underestimated and why queer Arab joy will always triumph.

These developments also allowed me to reflect on how queer Arabs find community and/or family (chosen or otherwise). This, in turn, allowed me to reflect on my own journey of seeking community and kinship with other queer Arabs.

It wasn't until my mid-twenties, shortly after my first serious relationship and several years after I started my coming out journey, that I truly discovered myself as a gay Arab in Sydney. Five years after that, I moved to London. Though I had a circle of friends in London and soon started dating the British man who would eventually become my husband, I still had to find other queer Arabs all over again. In my third year in London, I discovered the Pride of Arabia parties and book clubs, which gradually snowballed into other queer Arab community events, WhatsApp groups and parties. I also met other queer Arabs through activism, forging comradeship through marching together in pro-Palestine protests, London Trans Pride and attending a vigil for Sarah Hegazy, the late queer Egyptian activist whose passing in exile had an emotional impact on queer Arabs worldwide.

I derived much strength and joy – depending on context – from these queer Arab friendships, both in Sydney and London. But all of this was thrown into uncertainty in early 2023, when I experienced sudden and complete hearing loss. That year, which I spent waiting to receive a cochlear implant, I realised just how important family, friendships and community are.

While my husband was a beacon of support and love during that time (as he is today), I still felt socially isolated. My hearing aid was no longer providing me with clarity in sound, so I avoided large social gatherings. I had fewer FaceTime calls with my family in Sydney, as I couldn't hear them clearly anymore. This took me to emotional low-points and made me reevaluate my relationship with my longtime deafness. I did not realise how much I would miss being involved in queer Arab community events and gatherings and how much I would miss existing in those spaces with ease and confidence in communication. And while my husband (who has the patience of a saint) was there for me and understood my needs,

I still missed being surrounded by my large, loud Arab family on the other side of the world.

The uncertainty of whether the cochlear implant would be successful made me fear that I may never again experience the queer Arab joy I derive from interactions with community or family. I underestimated my need for these interpersonal dynamics, and the role my culture and sexuality played in that need.

Thankfully, after my cochlear was activated in the first week of 2024, my life quickly changed in the best way possible. It took a year of complete deafness to reflect on my journey seeking queer Arab community on opposite ends of the world. That year was a humble reminder to never take community for granted. It taught me how to celebrate our lived experiences with newfound appreciation.

There is an abundance of joy in queer Arab families and communities. Sharing that joy asserts our existence in cultures – both Western and Arab – that want to erase us. This joy deserves to be highlighted and celebrated. This joy proves that despite all the hardships we may experience, we are family, too.

SHROUK EL-ATTAR

DANCING QUEER

'You need to focus,' I have been told. 'Pick a direction.' And I agree, for the most part. But how can I strip away the parts of myself that don't fit the mould? How can I tell the story of how I became an engineer without mentioning the belly dancing? Without challenging what a 'real engineer' is supposed to look like, or what they're allowed to do? I'm not just one thing. I'm queer. I'm Arab. I'm an engineer. I'm a dancer. I refuse to cut myself into pieces just to fit. Because it's in our full, complicated selves that real strength lives. That's what makes a family resilient. That's what makes a story worth hearing.

When my family was deported, I lost more than just a home; I lost the certainty about who I could become. Two defining pursuits began to shape my life during those turbulent years.

The first was engineering. Here, I reflect on the challenges faced by the global ethnic majority and immigrants trying to break into the field, and how every 'no' I received only fuelled my determination to find another way forward. That fire didn't come from nowhere, it came from watching my family rebuild from nothing, again and again. I wanted to create stability, not just for myself, but to honour their strength and sacrifice.

The second was Dancing Queer, a project that began as personal resistance and blossomed into cultural reclamation.

Belly dance had been appropriated, distorted into a colonial fantasy stripped of its history. But for me, it was joy and power, a direct connection to my roots. In my performances, I wore sequins like armour, moving my body in defiance. When I danced, I wasn't just performing – I was remembering. I was rewriting. Each move was loudly declaring that I am still here. And I take up space on my own terms.

The moment I fused my passions, creating a non-binary, belly-dancing robot was electrifying. It felt like tearing down a wall that had no right to be there in the first place. For the first time, I wasn't switching between selves, I was building a world where all of me could exist at once, unapologetically.

This wasn't just a technical project; it was my rebellion, coded in circuits and hardware. This robot challenged the rigid norms of gender and reclaimed authenticity, merging cutting-edge technology with the elegance of traditional Egyptian dance. But I didn't wake up dancing.

I bolt upright to the shrill ring of my phone in the darkness. It's 5.00 AM. Who could possibly be calling now? For a moment, nothing makes sense. The room is unfamiliar, the shapes in the dark all wrong. Then it hits me, I'm not at home. I'm at my friend's place, curled up in their spare room. The call keeps ringing. My heart hammers as I fumble to answer. Before I can speak, my mother's voice bursts through, high-pitched and cracked with terror. 'They're here! They're breaking in!' she screams. In the background I hear the horrible sounds of heavy footsteps and chaos. For a split second, I am frozen, the world tilting under me. Then adrenaline floods my veins. I throw on yesterday's clothes with trembling hands and tear out of the flat.

I leap onto my bicycle and kick off so hard the pedals nearly snap. *Please, please, please let them be okay*, I chant in my head as I fly through the silent pre-dawn streets. The air is raw and cold against my face, each gulp of breath burning in my lungs. My phone is still in my pocket, chiming incessantly with incoming messages, but I don't stop to check it. I don't even notice my friends who are racing over in cars and on bikes a short distance behind. The blurry edges of sleep are still clinging to my eyes and all I can see is the road ahead lit by my swerving headlight. I run a red light at an empty intersection, legs pumping, panic propelling me forward. The city is quiet – too quiet – as if holding its breath for what I'll find at home.

Turning onto my street, I instantly know something is very wrong. The usually dark row of houses is awake with lights and movement. Neighbours stand in clutches on the sidewalk in robes and slippers, their faces pale beacons in the gloom. I skid to a stop and nearly fall off the bike. There's our small, terraced house halfway down the street, front door wide open, swinging back and forth in the wind. Every few seconds it bangs against the wall with a hollow thud. Our belongings are scattered across the front steps and path – a patchwork of clothes, books and personal items tossed haphazardly; glass shattered. Oh God. My stomach lurches. The early morning drizzle has turned into a cold, needling rain, which pinpricks my skin as I drop my bike and run.

Inside, a nightmare has come to life. The narrow hallway is strewn with shoes and jackets pulled from the coat rack. I stumble over an overturned Moroccan sofa cushion – one that used to sit proudly in our living room, now thrown to the floor, its embroidered patterns catching the harsh beam of a flashlight left on the side table. The walls, adorned with my mother's beloved glittered rose decorations, flicker in and out of shadow as figures move through the rooms. Those glitter roses – usually so warm and cheerful, sparkling in the light – now seem garish against the silhouette of a tall man in a helmet. I catch a whiff of something familiar and disorienting: Turkish coffee. In the kitchen to my left, I see a mug of my mother's morning coffee, still half-full, now stone-cold, next to the sink. Beside it, a dark liquid pools on the linoleum – a spilled drink, tea or juice maybe, knocked over. The sight of that small, ordinary mess amid the wreckage makes my chest twist. This was our home just minutes ago – peaceful, safe, waking up to a new day – and now it's been turned upside down.

A uniformed officer shoulders past me in the hall, nearly knocking me into the wall. I press myself back, heart pounding, as more border police flood our tiny living room. They're wearing bulky black bulletproof vests with bold letters across the front, helmets with visors, and heavy boots that stomp on our fraying rug. Their presence is overwhelming, a swarm of dark-clad figures moving with militant precision in the confined space. One of them barks orders into a radio. The walls seem to close in, the air thick with sweat and aggression. I struggle to breathe; it's as if their collective anger is sucking the oxygen out of the house. 'Where is my family?!' I shout, but my voice comes out strangled, unheard in the commotion. I feel invisible, a ghost in my own home as these intruders tear it apart.

Over the clamour, I hear a whimper from outside – my little brother. I spin on my heel and sprint back toward the open door, where the rain hits me full in the face. There, in the driveway, two officers are dragging my mother and my brother towards a black van parked at the curb. My mother's hair is loose and wild in the wind and her feet are bare on the wet concrete. She's in her thin nightgown, the one with the sunflowers, now soaked through and clinging to her shivering form. My brother, only sixteen, isn't even wearing a coat – just a t-shirt and pyjama bottoms. My chest constricts. I scan frantically for my sister – she's only seventeen. We were close in age. I was just nineteen myself, but in that moment, it felt like I should have been older, stronger, someone who could protect them. The van's rear doors open. In the dim light, I catch a glimpse of a terrified face pressed to the window: my sister is already inside.

'Mama! Ibby!' I scream for my mother and my brother into the stormy air, my voice cracking. My legs feel like they're moving through wet cement, everything in my body strains to reach my family. An officer steps into my path out of nowhere, a towering wall of black uniform. I collide with his solid form. His hands grip my shoulders with iron force, holding me back.

'Stay back!' he snaps, shoving me away as if I'm the threat. I stumble and fall hard on my knees on the pavement. Pain shoots up my legs, but I barely register it.

'Please, don't take them,' I beg, my voice raw and high like a child's. My mother hears me and twists her head around. Our eyes meet for one agonising second. Her face is streaked with rain and despair. She tries to say something, but an officer pushes her into the van, cutting her off. My little brother is wailing openly now, resisting with all his small might as they put him in the van after her. This cannot be happening. It feels like some horrific dream, a movie scene, not our life.

A wave of border police stomp through our tiny house, their voices cold, authoritative, final, as if we are criminals. There is also translator standing detached from the scene, relaying my mother's screams and my little brother's sobs into neutral tones, something digestible for the system that is destroying us.

Do you realise how fucked up that is?

Someone standing there.

Calmly translating our terror into bureaucratic language.

Making it legible for the system destroying us.

Do you really realise how fucked up that is?

The van's doors slam shut with a dreadful finality, swallowing my family whole. I lunge forward again, but two officers block me. This time a friend grabs my arm too, trying to save me from myself. I hadn't even noticed my friends arriving – one of my best friends is here in her hoodie and sandals, face soaked, having run through the rain behind me. Another friend's car is idling on the curb, headlights cutting through the grey dawn. Inside, I think I hear my brother screaming for me. I am failing them. 'STOP! Please!' I howl. One of my friends tries to wrap their arms around me from behind in a desperate hug, but an officer forcefully separates us, shoving my friend away.

'Get back, all of you!' she growls. My friends are shouting too – some at the officers, some encouraging me to step away – but I barely comprehend the words over the van's engine and my own heartbeat thundering in my ears.

The van begins to move, something in me shatters. A scream rips from my throat – a raw, animal sound that I didn't know I could make. 'No, no, no.' It's all I can say, over and over, a mantra of denial. I claw at the wet concrete, as if I could dig through it and somehow tunnel to wherever they're going. I am dimly aware of my friends hovering near me, of one kneeling down and putting a hand on my back, sobbing herself. Another friend is yelling curses at the retreating convoy through his tears. The officers form a loose line between us and the departing vehicles, stern faces impassive under their helmets.

After what feels like a lifetime, the flashing lights recede and the street falls quiet. The neighbours are watching, a few with phones out recording or calling someone, others whispering to each other with horrified expressions. With the authorities gone, my friends can gather around me without being shoved away. One friend drapes their dry coat over my shoulders and gently urges me to stand, but I can't yet. My gaze drifts behind me through our front door, still ajar. The house is a wreck, violated and empty.

It's illegal to detain children in the UK, so they call what just happened a 'Family Pre-Departure Accommodation' operation – such a sterile, deceptively warm phrase. They dare to use the word 'family' as though there is comfort in that cage. There's nothing accommodating about where they're taking my little brother and sister. It's a detention centre with pretty branding, where children are detained with cameras watching their every move, day and night. Privacy and dignity are stripped away along with shoelaces and personal belongings. The bitterness rises in my throat like bile. Our asylum claim was still being processed. We had a court date scheduled, just a few weeks away. But the Home Office stormed our home anyway, tore my family from our beds before sunrise and treated us like criminals before the system had even heard our case. We weren't protected. We weren't believed. We were disposable.

The last officer on the scene approaches me. He has removed his helmet, revealing a pale face with tired eyes. For a second I think I see a flicker of pity. He clears his throat and speaks in a clipped tone. 'We'll ... uh ... we'll arrange to send along your family's belongings. They won't be left with nothing.' His words are meant to sound reassuring, I suppose. As if any of this is reassuring. I stare at him, unable to form a reply. My friends murmur angrily behind me and the officer quickly steps back and turns away, adjusting the strap of his vest. I don't believe him. I don't believe a single hollow word. Those bags and clothes scattered in our hallway, the books and toys – they are pieces of our life, treated like rubbish. I know we will never see those things again. The authorities took my family, and with them they have taken everything that mattered. Promising to send our belongings is just salt in the wound, a meaningless courtesy that will never materialise.

What good is a box of our stuff without my family here to hold it?

The officer jogs off to join his colleagues in their cars. The street is dark except for the amber glow of a streetlamp reflecting on the pavement. My friends don't know what to say or do. None of us do. I turn toward the house, once warm with laughter, scented with my mother's cooking, cluttered with our silly arguments and midnight snacks and music. Now it's a crime scene. My brother's favourite football t-shirt is lying in a puddle of spilled tea. I choke back a sob as I pick it up and clutch it to my chest. My friends quietly follow me in, careful where they step. I sink onto the sofa, the same spot where Mama loves to sip her coffee in the mornings. The cushion is damp – either from the rain or someone's spilled drink – and it emits the faint scent of my mother's perfume. My friends sit with me, one rubbing my back softly, another holding my hand. They are whispering words of comfort: 'we're here.' 'We'll fight this.' 'You're not alone.' But I feel utterly alone. Outside, I hear the distant wail of a siren as the convoy carrying my family disappears into the city, into whatever hellish 'accommodation' awaits them.

Anger starts to simmer beneath my despair, hot and sharp. I was nineteen years old and I had been staying at a friend's house that night. Families shouldn't be ripped apart like this. My family is not a threat; my mother was making coffee, for God's sake, probably about to wake my siblings for school. Still, the cruel absurdity of it all makes my blood boil. They call it procedure; they call it the law – but I call it what it is: inhuman.

I open my eyes and look around at the friends gathered in our ravaged living room. They look back at me and I know they feel this outrage too. We exchange nods, silently agreeing we will not let this break us. Though my hands are still shaking, I wipe my face and sit up straighter. The urgency of the morning's terror has passed, leaving a heavy, aching resolve in its place. I know the fight isn't over. It's only just beginning.

In this quiet moment, as dawn's weak light starts creeping through the doorway, I allow myself to sob in the arms of the people who stayed by my side. Desperation, injustice, trauma – the weight of it all presses down on me. My family's footprints are still wet on the floorboards. They should be here. This is home and home is where your family should be.

Slowly, I stand and walk to the doorway again. The rain has eased to a mist and dawn is breaking – a bleak, grey morning over our shattered world. I step outside, my friends close around me, and together we watch the sun rise. I don't know what comes next, or how I will get through it, but I know one thing as sure as I feel the blood throbbing in my temples: this is the day everything changed. I will carry the desperation, the injustice and the trauma of it forever, fuel in my veins to fight for them.

I step onto a stage made of discarded pallets, hand built on top of cracked concrete and held together in parts by some duct tape.

It's not a theatre. It's an abandoned building we reclaimed. Cleaned, wired, lit up with fairy lights and too many extension cords. We used to hold gigs here, benefit nights to raise money for causes no one else would fund: imprisoned human rights activists, refugees denied legal aid. We danced, we sang, we yelled into microphones with fury and hope. Tonight, it's my turn.

My costume is red. Not off-the-rack red, Frankensteined red. I made it from Halloween scraps picked out of second-hand bins. The top barely matches the skirt, and there are threads unravelling at the seams. But it shimmers. It shimmers like it knows it wasn't supposed to exist. It clings in places I didn't plan, sparkles in places that demand attention. I made it. That's enough.

I haven't danced in a year. Not since the Home Office tore my family away and I stopped answering messages and began avoiding eye contact in the street, in case someone asked, 'how's your mum? How are your siblings?' Not since I began sleeping with shoes on, just in case.

The beat starts. The darbuka hits me like a memory in my chest, hips and jaw. It's not choreography or a routine. It's ancestry – I'm Egyptian. This rhythm lives in me.

We don't call it belly dance in Egypt, we just call it dancing. It's just how people dance. The Western expression belly dance is a distortion, a fantasy – the name for a harem delusion imported, exoticised and sold back to us like it was a gift. They grouped North African and Southwest Asian dances into a single term, flattened their differences, sexualised the whole lot and named it after a body part we barely use when we dance. What we do is hip work. It is history.

I also know the history of the glittery two-piece suit I'm wearing. Sabiaa Mesbahani, a genius businesswoman in Egypt of Moroccan origin, saw the look of disappointment on Western tourists' faces when they arrived in Egypt expecting harem fantasies and found male dancers, or women in full-coverage costumes. So, she gave them what they wanted: a costume inspired by Western burlesque. And with it, she sold them Egyptian dance and she profited from it.

It's a strange legacy, weaponising the male gaze to survive colonisation. But if you're going to be objectified, you may as well send an invoice. I kept the sequins. But I added something: a beard. Sometimes it was painted, sometimes glued on, some parts real. The beard changed night to night. From the moment I first wore it on stage, the room cracked open. Not literally – though the building did have loose bricks. It startled people. Not because it was a gimmick, but because it was a truth. I loved that.

Beards don't belong to masculinity and femininity doesn't have to be smooth. Plenty of cis women grow facial hair and are shamed into hiding it. Historically, Egyptian dancers were men, women and everyone in between. The term khawal, used today as Egypt's most cutting insult for a gay man, used to simply mean a male dancer. A gender non-conforming artist – someone like me.

The colonisers came, rewrote queerness as deviance and made khawal a curse. But I'm taking it back. On stage, with hips and hair and sequins and sweat.

If my beard makes you uncomfortable – good.

If you find it attractive – good.

If it makes you question what you desire – excellent.

That night, as I danced, I disappeared into the red lights. There must have been other colours, but red is all I remember. Red light. Red cloth. Red blood humming in my ears. I didn't see or hear the crowd until the end, when the music stopped and they erupted in cheers.

Later, I'd dance in shops and markets, at community events and queer fundraisers. And I'd see the difference. In some rooms, they cheered. In others, they averted their eyes or leered too long. The average everyday British politeness couldn't cover the discomfort. I wasn't palatable. I wasn't what they expected. Some men looked away as if that was respectful. Some men didn't look away and that was worse. It's in that tension, between disgust and desire, that Dancing Queer was born. Not just a performance, it's a dare. It's a refusal. What started as me sweating under red lights, became a movement. Dancing Queer is a living protest in sequins and circuitry. It's drag meets robotics, SWANA rhythms meets soldering irons. It's queer Arabs building stages where none existed, spinning joy from scraps and rage from wire. We perform in squats and galleries, in markets and museums. We run workshops where kids learn to code and shimmy at the same time. We make art that confuses people. And if it doesn't confuse them, it's not finished.

We're not here to entertain. We're here to rewire what visibility looks like.

I wanted my performances to do more than provoke:

I wanted them to protect. I set aside a portion of every gig fee for queer Egyptians, for shelter, legal aid and survival. Eventually, it grew into a movement and became a charity – the Shrouk El-Attar Trust. Because if I'm going to dance for you, you'd better know exactly who I'm dancing for.

But Dancing Queer didn't just help others survive, it helped me survive too. When the Home Office tore my family away, I was left trying to fill a silence that felt too big to carry alone. Dancing Queer became a lifeline. Through it, I found my people – trans folk, brown queers, asylum seekers, punks, artists, dreamers – who held me when I couldn't hold myself. We built something together, not just art, but kinship. Not just performances, but a kind of family that chose each other over and over again. Someone gave me a massage the week I stopped speaking. Others brought food when I forgot how to feed myself. They sang for Dancing Queer, danced beside Zooka, my dancing robot creation, in underground gigs lit by fairy lights and rage. And when it was all slipping through my fingers – when the admin, the funding, the exhaustion started swallowing me whole – Nadia caught it. Nadia wouldn't let it die. She emailed, she rallied, she filled out forms I couldn't face. She refused to let Dancing Queer be forgotten, even when I was too tired to remember it myself. That's what Dancing Queer gave me, not just a stage, but a family. One I chose. One that chose me back.

My love for engineering didn't start with a lab coat or a soldering iron. It started with a lie: that the people inside the television were real. I believed that, until I didn't. I realised those moving pictures came from circuits, logic and magic built by humans. I didn't know it was called electronics – but I knew I wanted to be the magician.

I started dismantling everything I could get my hands on: radios, toys, remotes, my mum's phone (that one didn't go down well). They never worked again, though I was trying to fix and understand them. One day, I told myself, I'll design something the whole world uses. Something they'll call magic without knowing it was mine.

Years later, I designed radiation-hardened PCBs (Polychlorinated Biphenyls – kinds of man-made, toxic chemical compounds) for NASA's lunar space station. I didn't arrive there with a scholarship and a smile. I arrived with scars, burn marks and teeth marks. And a mouth that had learned to swallow rage.

I struggled at school. Not because I wasn't smart, but because the system wasn't built for people like me. My ADHD and autism went undiagnosed. I was labelled difficult, lazy and disengaged. But my mum saw me and got me private tutors. My nights were spent studying with them, after full days of school. Exhausting? Yes. But it worked and I shot ahead. I skipped two grades. To everyone out there struggling: you're not stupid – you're just poor. Or misread. Or both.

In Egypt, where I did my early schooling, as many girls studied engineering as boys. The UK likes to act progressive, but Egypt schooled it when it came to that. Everything collapsed in 2007, when my family became refugees overnight and fled to the UK. We weren't running from war, we were running from my father. A man with friends in the Mubarak regime. A man whose power came not from status, but from silence. The silence of police officers who laughed off bruises and broken bones. The silence of neighbours who looked away. Even the silence that we ourselves were taught to keep from a young age. My mum reported him countless times. She ended up in hospital with broken bones, again and again. The police always took his side, even covered for him. We, the children, stopped flinching. We stopped asking questions. We thought that was just what families were.

My mum fled with nothing but survival in her hands. We arrived in the UK and were dropped into the asylum system. We lived in government housing for asylum seekers. I shared a room with strangers. I was allowed £5 per day to cover food, bus tickets, clothes, menstrual pads and painkillers. No wifi – that was considered a luxury. I wasn't allowed to work. I wasn't allowed to travel. I wasn't allowed to hope.

But I still had my maths. I'd already studied university-level material. When I sat my A-levels in the UK, I crushed them. I received full marks in two of three maths papers and one of the highest scores in the country. I applied to university aged fifteen and got in everywhere. But the system struck again. They classified me as an international student, though I was trapped in the UK (they took away my passport). As an international student, the fees were £25,000+ a year. As an asylum seeker, I had no access to loans or grants and I was not allowed to take a job.

I joined Student Action for Refugees. Three times, I stood in Parliament and demanded justice. We changed the policy – if you were born and schooled in the UK, you could now be classified as a home student. Thousands benefitted, but not me. We fought for Syrian refugees to get home status. Thirty thousand lives changed. Still not mine.

We turned to universities and, one by one, we got them to treat asylum seekers fairly by adjusting fees and offering scholarships. Over eighty out of 100+ universities signed on. We made change, but it was too late for me. By the time that door opened, my family had been torn from me and I was alone in the UK. I couldn't get out of bed. I couldn't face people asking how I was. When my asylum claim was finally granted, I didn't feel relief, I felt sick. Was I meant to celebrate this ... now? Now I could go to university? After everything?

I made myself get up. I applied to Cardiff University – only Cardiff. I couldn't leave the city. I couldn't handle another loss or another new place. My grief had built a shell around me and I didn't have the strength to shed it.

On my first day at university, I walked through the halls, students buzzing around me like static, laughing, shouting and living. I looked at them and thought: you have no idea what it took for me to be here. The sounds became too much. The colours were too bright. I had a meltdown on my first day. They said it was a panic attack. Later, a psychiatrist diagnosed me with ADHD. No one said autism yet – I wouldn't be diagnosed for another decade.

I told my youth worker, excited, 'now I understand why I struggle to start tasks even when I love them!' She told me, 'everyone's getting diagnosed these days.' My smile dropped. I started pretending to fit the ADHD stereotype and the cycle of doubt and dismissal continued.

University was hard. I only briefly had access to ADHD meds. Ever since we became asylum seekers, my mother couldn't afford private tutoring for me. And now that I was in the UK all by myself, I certainly couldn't afford any either. I had to move for a placement, which meant switching NHS catchment areas, which meant losing my prescription. I couldn't organise myself without meds, but couldn't get meds without organising myself. I got a placement, a software role, even though I'd studied hardware. The guy beside me had studied software. He got the real tasks and I got the scraps.

As an undiagnosed autistic person, I didn't know I struggled with indirect requests. I didn't know the manager saying, 'this needs doing' meant 'you need to do this'. When it didn't get done, I looked lazy and disobedient. They pulled me off important work.

When I returned to university for my final year of my bachelor's, I was assigned lead on group projects. I set deadlines and I followed up. I was called naggy. The autistic boys who barely spoke? Gifted. Precise. Brilliant.

Still, I kept going. I completed my degree and moved on to postgraduate studies. My master's project lit a fire again. I created a machine that could detect organic compounds – including some types of cancers – using electron quantum spin. Real innovation. Real tech. My kind of magic. I got my first real engineering job and I was buzzing.

The industry was still poisoned. A physicist told me, with a straight face, that men's brains are built for maths. 'It's science,' he said. Another told me that the pay gap wasn't real. A third smiled like he was complimenting me. 'It's real, but that's just because women are too smart to work as hard as men.' I complained and Human Resources asked why I'd brought up such a controversial topic, as if I was the problem.

I joined a FemTech engineering company where I thought I was safe and seen. A couple of years later, I found out a colleague – a man whose entire engineering career was shorter than the time I'd already spent just at that company – was earning more than me. Instead of rebuilding myself again in the industry's mould, I rebuilt on my own terms. I opened my own company. One that didn't just build electronics – it built possibilities. I helped other companies take their ideas and turn them into real, manufacturable products. I finally stepped out of the rooms that wanted me silenced and into a space I created and owned.

Still, I was split. Shrouk the engineer. Shrouk the dancer. Shrouk the refugee.

So, I did what engineers do when the blueprint doesn't fit: I made my own. The non-binary, belly-dancing robot wasn't a toy, it was a declaration. It danced Egyptian. Not the colonised, belly-button-fetishised fantasy, but real dance with hip work, rebellion and sequins and sensors.

It had gender and didn't. It shimmered and moved and asked questions simply by existing. It stands just under a metre-and-a-half tall and looks like patchwork joy, built from brightly coloured, Lego-like panels, stitched together like a queer Frankenstein in sequins. Its body is mounted on tank treads and under the skirt, it's all motors, wires and code. I used Arduino to power it – not because that's the limit of my skills (I build far more complex systems professionally, running the Zephyr real-time operating system and beyond), but because I wanted others to be able to build their own. I wanted this to be a blueprint, not a trophy.

At first, my mum wanted nothing to do with it. The dancing embarrassed her. The queerness frightened her. The robot confused her. She'd say, 'what will people think?' And for a while, the silence between us said everything. She was still in Egypt – deported and watching from afar. I was in the UK, never allowed to return. She was never allowed to enter. We haven't been in the same room since. If I get married, she can't come to the wedding. If she ends up in hospital, I wouldn't be allowed to be by her side. That border isn't just a line – it's forever.

And yet, somehow, across the distance, through second-hand stories, low-bandwidth clips and whispered updates passed between relatives, she saw me.

The performances kept coming. The workshops, the stages, the people moved to tears. My mum kept watching, quietly, from the corners of the Internet.

Then one day, without warning, she named the robot Zooka. Just like that. Like it had always had a name. Like she'd been thinking about it all along.

Now, my mother tells people I'm a fighter. A performer. An inventor. She tells them my robot's name with pride in her voice. Zooka is a tribute to what we survived, to what I built from it and to the quiet revolutions that happen in kitchens and phone calls and mothers' hearts.

You'll find Zooka and I performing at queer clubs, activist festivals, tech conferences and DIY gigs, wherever there's space to shake things up. Maybe it's opened doors, maybe it hasn't. But it's opened eyes. Children have come up to me and asked, 'can I build one too?' That's enough for me.

At a time when systemic barriers excluded me from the field, I found empowerment in sharing what I loved. Teaching engineering wasn't just about circuits and systems; it was about showing children, children who were just like me, that their curiosity mattered, even when the world told them otherwise.

I had never been taught engineering by someone who looked like me. Never by someone with a name like mine, skin like mine, a story like mine and certainly never through a decolonised art form like Egyptian dance. So, I became the person I'd needed and brought a robot with me.

We'd roll Zooka into classrooms where the heating was broken and the whiteboards were cracked, into youth clubs with sticky floors and ceiling tiles hanging loose. The robot's sequins caught the light, sometimes from a bare bulb, sometimes from a disco ball someone forgot to take down. Kids stared. Some laughed. Some whispered. But always, one of them, usually the quietest one, would edge forward and ask, 'is it allowed to do that?' Meaning:

Is it allowed to dance? To shine? To be weird?

Is it allowed to Arab?

Is it allowed to *queer*?

And I'd say yes. Not just because it's allowed, but because it's necessary. Because the blueprint these children have been handed doesn't include joy, glitter or defiance. But if I can rewrite my blueprint, so can they.

At performances, when people stared, I stared back. When they asked, 'why would you build this?' I said, 'because I needed to see someone like me'.

Because the industry tried to erase me.

Because queerness can compute.

Because engineering can dance.

Because I'm still here.

ZEID AL-NASR

ONE WAY TRIP TO THE MOON: MY JOURNEY WITH ONLYFANS

My mother used to tell me that if I were to leave home and abandon religion, or 'choose homosexuality' over my family, then I would need to change my name. She didn't want me to damage the family's reputation. And so, I did. I chose to name myself Zeid Al-Nasr. I wanted a name that started with the letter 'Z' – the last letter of the alphabet and the opposite of what my real name started with, 'A'. Al-Nasr is Arabic for 'victorious', a nod to the trials I experienced as a queer Syrian paving his own path in life.

Changing my name felt liberating. Carrying the family's name had become a burden I couldn't stand anymore. But while my new name gave me some newfound freedom, I now carried the weight of two separate lives: my past self and Zeid, the new digital persona I had begun nurturing on OnlyFans, where I used the username 'zeidmoon'. I had no idea that OnlyFans would change my life. I had no idea that zeidmoon would become more than just a username either, but it soon became a symbol of my transformation, representing what it meant to take control of my own narrative.

In a way, my mother's warning about changing my name

became a self-fulfilling prophecy, but not in the way she had thought. It was not a mark of shame. It became a badge of independence, a symbol of how I had chosen my own path despite the cultural, familial and global pressures trying to hold me back. Timing was on my side: I changed my name at the start of the pandemic. Despite everything, it was a good time for me to start over. A new world was unravelling and I needed to know what it could look like for someone like me. I looked at the uncertainty I was faced with as an opportunity for liberation.

I have always lived with uncertainty and often, between worlds. I grew up between Saudi Arabia and Syria. My siblings and I spent half of the year with our dad in Jeddah and the other half with our mum in Damascus. My parents planned that we would attend university in Syria once we finished school in Saudi Arabia. This came around for me in 2011, the year I turned eighteen and graduated from high school. I was ready to enrol at university to study psychology, but this was against my father's wishes – he thought working as a psychologist was a feminine career. We grew up religious. My father was traditional and believed in defined gender roles. He wanted me to study engineering, although I had no interest in that. The more he tried to push me into gendered roles, the more I wanted to break free from them. I went ahead and registered to study psychology. My father cut me off financially and told me that I was on my own and must provide for myself. I was determined to prove I didn't need his help, so I got a job in Damascus as an English teacher to kindergarten children. This enabled me to pay rent and monthly expenses while I pursued my university studies. I had a plan. I genuinely thought I would spend the rest of my life in my home country, because it's all I ever knew. I understood that this would mean forgoing my freedom as a queer man, but I felt safe at home.

That dream was crushed when the war started in Syria. What began as a student protest in a small town became a nationwide crisis. Weeks of protests turned to months of violence and the prospect of peace drifted further away each day. It was a strange time to live in Damascus. Fear roamed the city, haunting us all. Walking the streets, not knowing who was your enemy and who was your ally, was horrifying. One night I was waiting outside my friend's home when a group of seven or eight men appeared out of nowhere, running towards me. I was petrified. Should I start running too? If I ran, would they think I was guilty of something? I held my breath for a few seconds that felt like a lifetime, but the men passed right by me and it was clear they were looking for someone else. Strangely, it didn't feel like relief at all. It was a stark reminder that danger lurked around every corner, waiting for someone. You could be walking home from university one day and the next, that route was a battleground. The randomness of violence became a daily reality in Damascus. Uncertainty became our only certainty.

Three years later, there was no sign of a resolution or end to the nightmare. My university had been bombed multiple times. The interruptions forced it to shut down completely.

The infrastructure of Syria was falling apart. I had no choice but to leave the country, like so many others. Many took a boat to escape, not knowing where the water was taking them. In late 2014, I went to the South African consulate in Damascus and asked for a meeting with the consul. South Africa and Syria have a great diplomatic relationship, and it happened to be one of the few consulates that remained operating during the war. I had nothing to lose, so I told him I was gay and that I needed to leave Syria. I asked for his help or at least, guidance. He took my passport and asked me to fill out a visitor's visa application.

A few weeks later, I got a call from the consulate asking me to pick up my passport. I had no idea what was going to happen. I was terrified. I picked up my passport and in complete shock, there it was: a tourist visa to South Africa, valid for two weeks. I borrowed money from friends and using that, alongside my savings, I booked my flight to South Africa. I applied for refugee status the moment I arrived there. I felt that this was the place where I would spend the rest of my life. Little did I know that this was the beginning of a different kind of war – one that took place inside of me.

I didn't expect the hardships that came with refugee status. I felt so estranged from this new world I had landed in. From the narrow alleyways of Old Damascus, where sunlight filters through carved wooden walls along ancient stone pathways, I had come to South Africa, a land of contradictions where stunning nature exists alongside harsh realities – a land that welcomed me with open arms and closed fists. I found myself lost between worlds: not yet South African, but no longer

Syrian. I didn't stand a chance of survival. Somehow, I lasted for five years as a refugee in South Africa.

My world has always felt like it was under threat – from growing up queer in Saudi Arabia and living through the civil war in Syria, to becoming a refugee. From the moment of arrival, I was already struggling in South Africa – I couldn't find justice in a society where queer refugees were marginalised twice over: first for being foreign and second for being queer. The system that promised protection became another maze to navigate. I couldn't get a permanent visa, I couldn't open a bank account and I wasn't able to build anything for my future. My legal status was perpetually in limbo, while my identity as a queer man became both shield and target. I worked in the food service industry for around three years. I moved from one coffee shop to another, desperately hoping I would be able to save enough money to study. The longer I worked in the food industry, the more I felt stuck in it.

I had hit a wall. I couldn't move forward. The door to the life I yearned for felt like it was closing on me. Thankfully, a friend I had met online introduced me to a platform that would turn things around for me – an online platform where followers pay a monthly fee to content creators in exchange for access to exclusive videos and photos (usually sexually explicit ones). My friend said that he was earning money through this platform, known as OnlyFans. This platform, my friend told me, does not know societal or religious laws. It's a different kind of wilderness; a digital one, where boundaries are self-defined and liberation takes on new meanings.

The prospect of exposing myself online brought up

conflicting emotions. I worried what people would think of me if they knew. I grew up in a place where societal and religious laws shaped our beliefs and what our lives could look like. After years of living outside of the Middle East, I still struggle with traditions that are engraved in me. We never wore short dresses – even as a man you are supposed to cover up and wearing shorts or sleeveless t-shirts was not welcomed. I still sometimes catch myself covering up or feeling shame about my body, even in spaces where I'm completely free to express myself. I was never a guy who took a lot of nudes.

But alongside a fear of judgement and consequences, this new career offered me a new life. OnlyFans could provide a respite from my financial instability and a chance to reclaim my narrative on my own terms. I had to join, though I was hesitant, scared about what this new world could do to me and my image. I decided to take the risk. I signed up.

I didn't think I was the kind of person that people wanted to see naked, let alone having sex. I'd never even recorded myself engaging in a sexual act before. The idea of having sex on camera felt like a nightmare to me; it went against the secrecy and discretion etiquettes I had been so used to. Having an alter ego helped a lot in two ways. Firstly, this character became a costume that protected me. Even though I was dressing down instead of covering up, zeidmoon was a shield. Slowly but surely, I started building confidence by showing off my body online.

Secondly, changing my identity felt like the only way I could protect my family and live freely at the same time. My mom repeatedly told me as I was growing up that everything

I did reflected on our family and affected how people viewed my three sisters. I felt that if they ended up unmarried or alone, it would be *my* fault. My mom grew up in Syria during the 1970s and that's all I need to know to make sense of the way she thinks and speaks – it's not her fault we live in a misogynistic world. I am not going to punish her for sharing what she thinks is right when it's all she knows. I understand that as problematic as that world is, it made her feel safe. The possibility that my family would find out about my new career became more likely as my social media numbers grew higher, not just on OnlyFans, but also on other social media platforms. I went through my accounts and blocked every single relative, even friends-of-a-friend-of-a-relative, because I just couldn't risk being found out.

The first few posts felt strange. I felt like I was acting or putting on a persona that wasn't me. I didn't want to reveal too much of my personality; I wanted to have control over something at a time where I felt like I had lost control of everything else in my life. I was determined to maintain some boundaries. Some followers would ask about my real name, my background, wanting to know more about the person behind the screen. I had to decide carefully what parts of myself to share. The irony wasn't lost on me – in trying to be authentic and open on OnlyFans, I had to keep certain parts of myself hidden. These boundaries kept shifting as I became more comfortable with this new chapter of my life. And as my income from OnlyFans grew, those boundaries shifted even faster.

A few months after I started earning money on OnlyFans,

I had saved up enough to leave South Africa and move to Canada, which offered a permanent solution to the fear of being sent home. Strong winds of change stormed into my life and I welcomed them, letting them sweep me off my feet. I didn't know where life was taking me, but I knew that I had to find out.

Becoming a somewhat-known figure in the queer community, at least among gay men, was frightening, but at the same time it helped me build my future. Prior to arriving in Canada, I had connections with members of the community in Toronto thanks to my online presence. I arrived in October 2020. It was a difficult time to move into a new place because of restrictions related to the pandemic, but luckily, many people knew about me, so I didn't feel like I was starting from zero. Online connections often transformed into real-life connections. Geographically speaking, Canada was even further away from Syria than South Africa, which helped me disassociate from the Middle Eastern world. This time, the move was different, more positive. I had some money saved and a steady income from OnlyFans. I had some connections and people wanted to meet me. I did not experience the hardships in Canada that I had experienced when I first moved to South Africa.

But my life was still a battle: between the person I was taught to be and the person I was choosing to become. I grew up in a place where secrecy and intimacy go hand in hand. As a queer person in Syria and Saudi Arabia, I had learned to hide to protect myself. Meeting guys for a date was not something I advertised in my old life. Back in the Middle East, when I met guys for dates, I lied to my high-school friends about having a girlfriend and I lied to my family that I was with my high school friends. Fear of being discovered, or outed on terms that were not my own, was ingrained in me. I had built a world of lies to protect myself and everyone around me from my sexuality.

But what used to protect me no longer worked in Canada. I had always thought that if I were to leave the Middle East to live my true authentic self, I would still live in the shadows. Yet if I wanted to survive and make a living in Canada, I needed to do the opposite. I had to blow my own cover to show off my sexuality and make a living. Recording myself felt like stripping away years of a carefully constructed façade. Here I was, stepping out deliberately into the light – a light that continued to shine on me even when the cameras were off.

I had no idea what I was doing on OnlyFans when I started. I knew people wanted to see more, but I didn't know what that meant. I wanted to do it my way – I knew what porn looked like and I knew I couldn't exactly do *that* and I didn't feel up to par with what was already on offer. I wanted to keep some form of privacy (I didn't know that wasn't possible). The more I posted content, the more my followers wanted to know about me. They wanted to know my story, where I came from and what brought me to OnlyFans. What I had initially begun to make money turned into something more personal.

My followers became invested in my journey – not just the explicit content, but the person behind it. They wanted to know about my experiences as a queer Arab immigrant, my thoughts on love and relationships and how I navigated these different worlds.

I also have many followers who aren't looking for intimacy. Catering to men meant that I needed to become a 'perfect' human with no insecurities about their body. Many men are after a standard of unattainable perfection that they project onto performers like me. In my experience, men don't like it when you reveal insecurities or show them weakness. I believe that insecurity and shame translate through everything – even digital screens – and I didn't want people to see through me like that. A lot of followers came to me because I was portraying strength and confidence, even though inside I was still battling my own demons. Many were drawn to this image of a strong, unapologetic queer Arab man who had overcome adversity. I really wanted this to be my reality and I knew that if I pretended for long enough, I would eventually believe in the image I created, too. I had to learn how to love my body in the same way that these people did.

A little over a year after I started doing OnlyFans, I had saved up enough money to pay for university in Canada. I began studying in autumn 2021. I was happy to pursue education again and I felt privileged to have that opportunity. I know so many people from back home who will never have the chance to study again. I didn't want to take all that I had for granted.

Returning to education gave me the drive to keep

performing online. When I started making porn, I knew that I didn't want to do it forever. But the money I earned allowed me to afford rent, tuition for my education and a life that I could never have dreamt of a year earlier. Not only was my work affording my basic survival, but now it was also helping me build for my future, something that no family member or job had ever provided before. It gave my career as a sex performer a new meaning and I started feeling proud of what I do. I finally felt like I had regained control over my life. I had reclaimed my power and I could shape my own story.

Unfortunately, along with the financial stability and a chance to imagine a future, OnlyFans also brought me a lot of anxiety. As my following continued to grow, the fear of being caught by my family also increased. The work was full time and required dedication, creativity and resilience. The emotional labour, constant content creation, and marketing and managing relationships with subscribers was anything but easy. I also worried, *how do I keep this up? How can I maintain what I have today?* I didn't feel like I deserved this success. I constantly felt like I was taking something that wasn't mine. I was terrified of losing it all, which had been a common theme in my life up to this point.

It didn't help that some people have preconceived notions about sex work, often viewing it through a lens of moral judgement or pity. A lot of people tried to shame me for using OnlyFans. The most common stigma that people have around sex workers or performers is that they are 'cash grabbers' – people who will do anything for a quick cheque. I was told my earnings were 'easy money' and that I wasn't really working hard for it. There are stereotypes that sex workers are either victims of circumstance or morally corrupt individuals. Even those who consider themselves progressive can perpetuate these stereotypes. But what most don't understand is that sex work can be a legitimate choice – one that allows people like me to pursue education, achieve financial independence and support others.

Meanwhile, I worried about my family's wellbeing, too. The more stable my life became, the less stable my family's life became back home. As the war and economic situation worsened in Syria, my family struggled with affording basic necessities. The guilt of having financial security while they suffered weighed heavily on me. I offered to send my family an allowance every month to help them cope with the skyrocketing costs of living. While it wasn't much by Canadian standards, the exchange rate meant I could make a big difference. My transfers started with small amounts of money and slowly these increased. With every problem or financial trouble they experienced, I was quick to offer my family help. In truth, much of this stemmed from a desire to ease my guilt about doing porn. My willingness to financially support my family in Syria helped to quiet the inner voice that made me feel ashamed about sex work. After years of chaos, there was finally some sense of balance to my life.

Then one day in 2021, I woke up to a phone call from my mom. My sister, who was twenty years old at the time – she is ten years younger than me – had become involved in an altercation with the police. She had been taken to jail because she had spoken up to an officer who harassed her and her friends at a park. My mom told me she had been hiding this from me for a few days hoping that she could fix it, but she couldn't. She needed my help.

I was in shock. I didn't know how to respond. None of our family members had been arrested before, let alone my little sister. My mom asked if I could send her money to hire a lawyer and to bribe prison guards to take better care of my sister. She said that a police officer promised to release my sister if they received a certain amount of money, but unfortunately that did not happen. It was one of the scariest times for us as a family. We didn't tell my dad for the first couple of weeks, hoping that my sister would be released before he had to know.

Weeks turned to months. We kept promising my sister it would be over soon, but we didn't know that. I was only able to speak with my sister once while she was in jail. It broke my heart to hear her voice, she sounded so defeated. All we could do was throw money at people to help us. Though none of it really seemed to work, we weren't going to stop trying.

The pressure intensified – I needed to create more content on OnlyFans, grow my income and increase the monthly allowance I was sending home. Every notification, every new subscriber became a lifeline to help my sister. My relationship with my work transformed again as did my relationship with my family. The power dynamic had shifted completely. I was no longer being asked questions about my life or where my money came from.

Almost a year after she'd been arrested, my sister was finally released from jail on probation. She was awaiting trial but thankfully she didn't have to stay in prison until the court date. We didn't know what was going to happen and we didn't really have hope or faith in Syria's justice system. We arranged my sister's paperwork and she escaped to Egypt. I was terrified, but I knew that using my newfound privilege to help ensure she was somewhere safe, away from the Syrian authorities, was the right thing to do. I had been around my sister's age when I left Syria for South Africa. I didn't want my sister to have to go through the same tribulations that I had. I truly wish that I had had someone at that time to rely on. I wanted to be the person that I never had, for her.

A few months after my sister arrived in Egypt, I encouraged her to pursue her education, hoping she wouldn't have to wait over a decade to get a degree like I did. She agreed. Once again, OnlyFans took on a new meaning – it wasn't just about my survival or education anymore, but about creating future opportunities for my sister, too.

My sexuality, which I was rejected and banished for, has become a lifeline for my family. I could be bitter about what I endured, but I could never punish my mom and three sisters for something bigger than they are. OnlyFans has become a bridge to education, support and personal growth. Sex work allowed me to support my family and become closer to them. What started as a means of escaping my family has become the thing that brought me back to them.

Unfortunately, our relationship remains complicated. Even though I am now a major source of relief and income for my family, we're still not open or honest about where the money comes from. They never ask and I never share. They don't want to be faced with an answer they don't like. If they knew, they would have to refuse it and even worse, refuse me. A huge part of navigating Middle Eastern cultures involves living in blissful ignorance – it's a place where things happen, but events aren't acknowledged or discussed openly. My family choosing not to question the source of my money is a perfect example of this unspoken understanding. It allows them to accept the help my mother and sisters desperately need while maintaining a façade of traditional values. In a way, this silent arrangement works for both me and my mother – I can support my family without explaining or justify my choices and they can receive the help they need without confronting realities that might challenge their beliefs.

To this day, I still find this dilemma and responsibility difficult to deal with. It pains me that I will never feel truly loved or accepted by my family. Though I want to believe that this wound of abandonment has healed and that I no longer care about my relationship with my family, I care a lot. Today I am a character to my family, just as I am a character to my online followers. I fulfil a role in their lives. I study what their needs are and I try to mirror them in a character that I believe they want to see in me. There's no place for my true, full self in my relationship with my family.

Through sex work, I've come to understand that choices and circumstances are far more nuanced than most people realise. My experience has shown me that sometimes the most unconventional choices can have the most meaningful impact.

OnlyFans allowed me to shape my own future and become the support system for others that I once desperately needed myself. Knowing yourself and staying true to who you are, underneath all the different façades that sex work and life may impose on you, is something I continue to learn every single day. Life is an endless process of learning and unlearning. I consider myself lucky to be able to see through that pattern. I understand that my identity is not measured by success, money or how other people perceive me. My identity, outside of zeidmoon and outside my real name, is unique and belongs only to me.

RANDA JARRAR

LEARNING FROM OTHER MOTHERS AT A TIME OF GENOCIDE

You are the mother of an adult Palestinian son. You raised him alone for years and, just as he is about to graduate from college, a genocide unfolds.

You are angry at the Zionist entity and its unapologetic slaughter of teachers, poets, garbagemen, cooks, soccer players, musicians, playwrights, nurses, doctors, actors, students, professors, writers, babies, toddlers, children, teenagers, elderly women, elderly men, disabled people of all ages. You don't sleep, but rest in spurts, monitoring the war crimes raining down on the innocent people in Gaza.

In a meeting with other Palestinian writer-mothers of the diaspora, one of you remarks that being away from Palestine and watching the daily horrors is akin to being chained in a room next door to a killing shed. You can see the people being killed in the space right next to you, you can bear witness and record what is happening for posterity, but you are powerless to actually stop it. This makes you angry, because you can't stop thinking of ways to stop it.

You meet with other queer comrades in community spaces,

leaving all your phones in faraday bags at the door. You all wear masks to maintain anonymity and because the pandemic never ended. You plan to shut down awards shows, embassies, roads and highways. You meet with people who, like you, are sick of seeing children ripped to shreds on their screens. You are also sick of how people use these children to convince other people that children should or should not be bombed. These children have names: Rana, Lana, Aya, Wateen, Tareq, Salma, Muhammad, Banan, Omar, Layan, Jannat, Misk, Bisan, Ayman, Naya, Juwan. They are human. UNICEF calls the genocide a 'graveyard for children'.

These children's mothers have names too. You are all tired of the ways these children and their mothers have become rhetorical tools.

Each person, you scream when you march together, each person is a whole world unto themselves. Each person had dreams and wishes and a voice. Each person was targeted inside a concentration camp they were not allowed to leave.

Together with your queer comrades, you block a highway, reminding each other to be like water. You must not be captured by the state. You must flow with each other away from surveillance.

You visit encampments, where students refuse to allow their universities get away with murder. You stand alongside them while racists firebomb students' tents, setting off fireworks to burn them out of their right to protest.

With your queer comrades, you attend talks with Zionists who think a ceasefire is out of the question. You play the names of the people murdered by Israeli and US-made bombs through a loudspeaker. Together, you scream at the racists until security carries you out of the hall by your chair, which you refused to get out of, forcing them to drag you. You are told by the attendees that they were just there to attend a talk. *They* were not aiding genocide. You remind them that people during Nazi holocausts also went out on cool, nice evenings to attend talks. Nothing about genocide, you remind them, is normal.

With your fellow disabled comrades, you visit weapons manufacturers around the Los Angeles area, struck by how banal the locations are: right next to a Taco Bell, a school or a Home Depot garden centre. Most of these buildings are secured by one person, usually a man, whose job it is to protect the workers inside, who make parts that go into bombs and missiles that tear apart children named Salma, Muhammad and Banan.

The actionists you attend meetings with tell you and each other that though evading arrest is important, it is not as important as dismantling these facilities. They remind you that spending a few months in prison for wrecking and possibly shutting down a weapons facility is a small price to pay for living in the core of empire and enjoying that empire's spoils while children like Jannat and Hind and Malak are killed in their sleep.

Many people in Gaza call you at all hours. When you video call them, you see their tents and the places where they sleep. They ask you to send money, explaining the ways the blockade has made the price of a tomato unaffordable. Mothers need diabetes medicine, menstrual pads, or the simple comfort of a blanket.

One day, at a protest, you meet a fellow Palestinian femme. She rides a motorcycle alongside the crowd, waving a Palestinian flag. Together, you come up with an idea to ask tattoo artists to hold a day for Palestine, where they each draw up a flash sheet of images to tattoo and they pledge to give 100 per cent of the money they make to a mutual aid fund. Hundreds of tattoo artists rise to the task, each of them once the child of a mother. In tattoo shops all over the world, people get inked with images of keffiyehs and tatreez. You get a tattoo too and while there, see that a young queer Latina has just got a fresh tattoo of the quote, 'soul of my soul', in Arabic and English. You think of Khaled Nabhan, the grandpa who became a social media personality after he was filmed uttering those words while holding his slain granddaughter, Reem, and weep.

Then, one afternoon, you attend a video call with a bunch of comrades who are in Cairo, aiding recent refugees from Gaza. You discover that there is a way out for many people who want to leave: a private company in Egypt called Ya Hala works with the Egyptian military to bring Palestinians in Gaza across the border and into Egypt, away from genocide. The company charges 5,000 US dollars for each adult and 2,500 US dollars for each child it helps save. You have complicated feelings about this: shouldn't organisations be helping people for free? And shouldn't indigenous people be able to live on their land in peace? But who are you to say they must stay there while you are living in comfort in Los Angeles?

The organisers helping to coordinate many of the families and their escape to Egypt are queer. You experience a deep sense of pride when you think of how many queer folks are helping Palestinians in Gaza. Queer communities excel at organising and collective care because we've had to. You understand that the body is a border and queer people understand this borderland existence. You navigate the spaces between acceptance and rejection daily, building community in the cracks of a system not designed for you. And there's something powerful about people who have been told they don't belong creating belonging for each other. You practice care as revolution. When you've been told your existence is wrong, simply creating space becomes radical. In sharing vulnerability, you go beyond survival and into transformation; the kind of deep love that crosses every border designed to contain it.

During the video call these new comrades appeal to everyone present to come to Egypt and help settle these families. There are mothers who need help with education, hospital stays, transportation, medical appointments, finding apartments and furniture; they need new clothes, new shoes, diapers, baby clothes. They also need people to fundraise and bring cash to help bring others out of Gaza.

Deciding to go to Egypt is the easiest decision you make.

You send a message to everyone you know, telling them you would like to raise 10,000 US dollars – the maximum amount of cash you are allowed to bring into Egypt at one time. You set aside the money in your savings account for helping Gazans in Egypt. Your queer friends – your chosen family – want to help pick up clothes to take. You print a form, listing the needs of one family comprised of a recently evacuated mother along with her husband, children and grandchildren. They are thirteen in total. The form includes their clothing and shoe sizes and their genders. You ask the organisers if it would make more sense to shop when you arrive, but they encourage you to shop in LA, as they are busy in Egypt working with people to secure hospital care, schooling, work and apartments, so the shopping there might take longer.

Your friend Kafiyah, a Sudanese organiser, sends you a giant suitcase for transporting the donated goods through your friend Taz, a Bengali artist and poet. Angela, a queer Filipinx poet and fellow creative writing professor, meets you for coffee and the two of you walk to a nearby shop to pick out some clothes for the adults in the family. Peering through racks of clothing, you try to find things that are modest and made of quality materials.

Your friend Dana, a Lebanese Egyptian perfumer, gathers materials for hygiene kits and puts them together in your living room. She helps you pack a bag of kits, and reusable menstruation pads and diapers, and zips up the bag that will miraculously go, through your friend Susan, who is a Palestinian writer, to Gaza.

Your friend Fawz, a queer Pakistani filmmaker, picks you up a few days later, since you don't have a car these days, and drives you to a big store where the two of you find children's shoes, period pants, reusable diapers, several pairs of sneakers, colourful kids' clothes, books and fun little jewellery kits. You both grieve that it is possible, in the same world, for you to walk safely through stores and purchase things for a family who, until recently, were denied access to the most basic hygiene products. You grab bottles of vitamins, worrying that the gelatine has pork in it. You pick out shoes that seem aesthetically pleasing as well as comfortable. Neither of you wants anyone who had to walk miles through a concentration camp to walk a single step in uncomfortable footwear.

Your community goes above and beyond and you raise over 20,000 US dollars for Palestinians to escape into Egypt, double the original target.

Unsure of how you will bring all that cash into Egypt, you ask friends to travel with you, but can't find anyone who can take time away from work. Instead, you strap 20,000 US dollars-worth of cash to your breasts and belly and take a flight to Cairo on Turkish Airlines (which you discover is sometimes called Turkish Hairlines because of all the men who take it to travel to Istanbul for hair transplants).

When you land in Cairo, you don't declare the cash. You take a taxi to an apartment you rented and write to Sara, who needs 5,000 dollars to evacuate her husband from Gaza. She and her children were able to escape to Cairo a few months ago and she hasn't been able to sleep since, worried about their father, her husband. You ask Sara to come over in the morning so you can give her the cash she needs. She is terrified that you are too good to be true, but says she will be there in the morning.

You wake up and wash your face and make tea and wait for her to arrive. When she appears in the apartment building hallway, you embrace her and invite her in. She tells you how her family escaped the morning of 8 October because they knew the Zionist army would rain hell on them. She tells you about the weeks she spent moving from evacuation zone to evacuation zone, until – by sheer luck – she finally found a way through the border. Her grandmother gave birth to her mother in Egypt many decades ago and because of that, her mother was eventually able to secure her an Egyptian passport, which she could then procure for her own children. The matriarchal luck her grandmother passed down to all of them and the small window through which the Egyptian government evacuated their citizens, regardless of their Palestinian ethnicity, kept her alive and her husband trapped inside the concentration camp that is Gaza.

You give Sara the cash, plus a bit more, so that she can set up a small apartment to welcome her husband and house herself and her children. She tells you that until that moment she was terrified that you were a spy or a human trafficker and that she had lost hope in all human beings. You tell her you don't blame her.

She shows you photos of her kids, zooming in on her favourite outfits and toys she had bought them in Gaza. She is heartbroken that she couldn't bring any of their things with her. She says she knows that things are just things, but she also feels that these clothes and toys she had bought them were expressions of her love and each outfit she had picked out for her children was meant to bring them joy. Now, they are blasted under rubble. Sara doesn't understand why children's clothes or toys deserve to be bombed. You don't understand it either and affirm her grief.

That afternoon, Sara leaves your rental, goes directly to the agency, files paperwork and pays for her husband's safe passage. Then, she waits. Evacuations often take as long as six weeks.

The next day, you visit your old teenagerhood best friends – twins you used to have a crush on. They are now mothers and you finally get to meet their kids. Their fathers are nowhere to be seen and the household is bustling with the sounds of cooking and video games. You tell your old BFFs that you are in love with your girlfriend and one of them says she's happy for you, while the other one is shocked that you have a girlfriend. You're gay? she says. Queer, you correct her, and she makes a face. Why do Americans have to have a word for everything? she says. You laugh and remind her that there are at least ten times as many words in Arabic as there are in English. Her sister is embarrassed and tells her to stop being ignorant. You tell them both you're not gay, as in only interested in women who identify as women, but queer, as in you identify as a pangender femme who is attracted to all genders. You see that the same twin is now very, very confused. You tell her you'll send her a book on gender and sexuality. Do you still read? you ask, knowing it sounds like a cunty question. You'll need to read up on it to support your kids, when they start having questions about these things, you say. Yes, the other twin says. Send it to both of us. You say you will. Pleased with yourself, you change the subject.

The following morning, you take a taxi to the temporary home of queer organisers who are planning the evacuation of more people from Gaza. You give them the rest of the cash and admire their small family of adopted kittens, street cats they have recently given a home to. The queers keep records of the family members they are trying to reach for evacuations. They place the cash you brought them into piles that they count out, delirious from a lack of sleep and nonstop dedication. You remind them that they need to rest. You are twenty years older than these wonderful people. You have experienced burnout many times, believing that you must be there to care for others, even if it means breaking your own back. You share as much wisdom as you feel they are capable of receiving.

That night you walk through the strangely quiet streets of Maadi, its trees wild and dusty, and arrive at the house of a writer who was evacuated after being captured by the Zionist forces. You meet his wife and children. His oldest daughter is ten years old and you give her a bracelet-making craft kit you bought her back in California. She asks you, excitedly, why your hair is shaved on the sides if you wear lipstick. You tell her it's because you like it and you want it to be shaved. She smiles, discovering something. The writer hadn't asked for much; just a card game he used to play with Refaat Alareer, which you'd found easily, and a wall calendar, which you hadn't. You had spent two days going from store to store, searching for a wall calendar. When you tell him this now and apologise that you couldn't find one, he says, your country is so strange. It commits genocide but has no wall calendars. You are sad because the USA is not your country.

His wife says that the first and most important thing to

do when Palestine is free is to set up schools for the children. You agree with her and listen as she passionately describes the curriculum she would want to implement. His daughter makes you bracelet after bracelet. When you have dinner with them all, his youngest tells Gazan rhyming jokes and the daughter keeps wanting your attention. When the writer tries to tell a story, she tells him boldly to shut up. Shut up, Baba! she says again. He is amused. You tell her she's very lucky that she can talk to her father that way. You say your father was once a poet but he didn't ever allow you to tell him what to do. She says, yes, but now you have the hair you want to have.

On one of your last days in Cairo, you visit the family you and your friends in LA had gone shopping for. One of the adult sons comes to meet you in the street outside the apartment and helps you with the large suitcase you brought them. He tells you right away in the elevator that he hates Egypt and misses Gaza. You affirm him and listen. In the apartment, the women of the family greet you while the men stay in a separate area. You love this so much, the way the mothers and their mother welcome you, give you tea and begin to tell you stories of their survival and their grief. The matriarch, the mother of them all, is a fat matriarch with masculine mannerisms and short hair. She wears a t-shirt and pants and sits on the only armchair, her throne. She regales you of stories about all the friends she lost in the previous weeks to bombings. She tells you about the son she lost years ago, during an older war – she calls them wars – when he was only seventeen years old. She tells you he was just playing soccer with his friends near the beach, and then he was gone.

Then she tells you how relieved she is that her best friend left Gaza with her. She says her best friend is in the first apartment the family fled to when they first left. She says the apartment you are in with her now is new and she's not sure she likes it, but she feels guilty, because she says her loved ones back home are disappearing, kidnapped by soldiers, and she shouldn't be picky about where she lives. Her best friend in the first apartment is her everything, she says. She is my friend, my sister, my mother and my lover. You pause for a moment, not knowing if you heard what you heard. You turn to the matriarch's daughters and they nod. They know. The matriarch tells you she wishes she could live with her best friend, but their families are too big, and one apartment is not large enough for twenty-seven people. You agree and you listen and she holds your hand and thanks you for bringing them gifts. The children and the women and the matriarch open the suitcase and begin distributing the clothes and the shoes and the other items they need. You are sad when they thank you again and tell them it is the least you can do.

A few days later, you come home to your girlfriend, who you love calling your wife, and your two dogs. You are so relieved and so grateful and so ready to keep working towards liberation. As a little girl, you once made a wish in a fountain to live with three girls. Looking at your wife and two female dogs, you cannot believe your luck.

A few weeks later, you must face the fact that your oldest

dog is dying. You have stopped counting her age properly. She was your child's stand-in after he moved away. Now, she is more like your grandmother than your child. Frequently, you have to feed her by hand. She is no longer in control of her bowels. When you put a nappy on her, she spends an hour kicking the nappy off, then soils every surface in your apartment.

She loves to walk around the living room all night and into dawn, trotting hurriedly but with no real destination. You don't want to accept that she's experiencing dementia. You don't want to name it as such. But it's true. She is no longer herself.

When you take her to the vet's office, you feel sad, because dogs in the USA have better healthcare than humans in Palestine, maybe even than humans in the USA. You admire the sleek reception area, the roomy examination spaces, the ease with which you can secure medicine for your dog.

Your girlfriend suggests visiting an animal communicator. You are unwilling to spend any money on anything so gay. You refuse to believe that a person who lives in another state has the ability to speak to your pet through a video call. Your girlfriend offers to pay for it.

Finally, you agree. The communicator asks for photos of your pet. You take them from several angles and every angle shows that your dog is incredibly elderly and beyond blind. You send the photos and get ready for the session, holding your girlfriend's hand and worrying about what might be revealed to you about your poor pet.

The communicator says that your dog is sad because you broke a pact with her. She doesn't need to say anything else;

you know what pact she's speaking of. When you first adopted your dog, the pact was that you would care for each other. But in the past few months, as the genocide in Gaza worsened and your dog's health has deteriorated, you have distanced yourself from her in order to make your parting more manageable. This was a mistake, your dog tells you through the communicator. She wants you to re-commit to caring for her, and caring for her includes allowing her to leave this earth with dignity. She doesn't want to pee in her own bed anymore. She doesn't want to trot around the apartment aimlessly and urgently, confused about where she's meant to be. She wants to be free.

You ask the communicator if your dog understands that you're Palestinian, if she understands that your people are being killed, starved, exterminated. Your dog says she does know and sees how much the pain affects you. Your dog says she wants to pass before the genocide gets worse. That is when you begin to cry. You had hoped that the killing would stop, not worsen.

You spend the next few weeks giving your dog her favourite foods, walking her in her dog stroller, a pink pram that gives her joints comfort while allowing her to sniff different scents at the park. When you are ready to say goodbye, you ask a vet to come to your home to help release her. You don't want her to die in a cold office.

The day the vet arrives, you give your dog some turkey, which she loves, and hold her on your couch. When the vet administers the anaesthetic, you feel your dog's body relax. When she received the second shot, you thank her and tell her you love her. You wrap her in a blanket and say goodbye. She is gone and your pact is complete. You weep, mourning the love you shared, a love you had never expected and will never forget. You weep, for all the people who lost their lives, for all the lives robbed of dignity in death, and for all the deaths you could not prevent.

ANDREW DELATOLLA & KARIM CHEDID

A FAMILY OF OUR OWN

When we first adopted our cat Othello in 2015, three years after we got together, Karim's mum joked: 'if the cat survives, will you graduate to a child?' That was the first time we talked about having children.

Both of us knew that we wanted to be parents. It was something we'd talked about early on in our dating and we were soon confident that we wanted to have that experience with one another. We had long conversations about what our future family could look like and how we would include our culture and heritage, but we didn't always agree on how we would get there.

For Andrew, adoption was the only avenue to grow our family beyond the two of us – and Othello, of course. He never felt a biological connection was necessary for our child to be closer to us, or better mannered or more stable. He was also concerned about the number of children already in the system and had ethical and moral qualms concerning surrogacy, especially gay surrogacy.

For Karim, the route to adoption was not as straightforward. Years after his mum first made her joke about our cat, but before the financial crash in Lebanon, she brought up the topic again, this time, with some insistence that she'd like to see our genes – or more specifically Karim's genes – passed on. Pushing for surrogacy, she suggested she'd pay if money was an issue (it wasn't). Her insistence on biological grandchildren haunted Karim, who clung to the Arabic expression '*yalli khallaf ma meit*' ('he who procreated did not die'), which is often said in solace at funerals. The saying insinuates that if your genes aren't passed on you die twice – you experience both your own death and then the death of your ancestors. This idea triggered Karim's guilt. Your family line. Cut off just like that. The tree with roots but with no branches.

There is a practice in Mexican culture whereby photos of those who have passed away are left out for others to see. The thought behind this tradition is that the more frequently we remember those who are gone, the more at peace the deceased will be in the afterlife.

The animated film *Coco* plays on this tradition. In the film, characters in the afterlife disappear once no one in the living world remembers them. Karim often thinks of *Coco*. And he often – on a daily basis – remembers, and dreams of, his grandmother, Téta Yvonne, who passed away sixteen years ago. How well she must be living in the afterlife, if her quality of life there is based on how frequently living people remember her! Legacy is stronger than genes. The people you've raised or have helped raise are part of your legacy. And it takes a village to raise a child – certainly where we come from.

Téta Yvonne used to say '*ma byetlaa jeel illa ma yhid jeell*'; 'a generation can't grow up without wearing out a generation before it.' We both admire the positivity this aphorism carries around legacy, of how it accepts mortality for what it is: the end of one life but not the end of a community. It celebrates community over self and how communal traditions and values live on. And doesn't that apply to anyone a person has touched in their lives, not just their biological relatives? It emphasises the communal nature of raising children. We came to lean on that perspective, instead of focusing on genetics. Perhaps the Arabic expression 'he who procreated did not die' needs to grow up too, to '*yalli rabba ma meit*' ('he who raised [someone] does not die').

Téta Yvonne also always told Karim that out of all her grandchildren, he's the one who would end up with someone from Marjeyoun, the southern Lebanese town less than 10 kilometres away from occupied Palestine, where both our families come from.

When we started chatting online in 2012, we had no idea what we were embarking on. Karim first messaged Andrew when he spotted the keffiyeh in Andrew's profile picture. Immediately, we challenged each other emotionally and intellectually. There was a spark in those first few weeks and there were also differences from the get-go – Karim was not very impressed with Andrew's views on the Middle East and vice versa.

Aside from our differing views, on a practical level, bringing our lives together has not been straightforward. We've navigated work crises, a long-distance relationship

(Andrew took a job in Cairo for nearly two years), the stress of buying and selling property (multiple times) and two house renovations, alongside negotiating family dynamics and expectations. At each turn, we have learned about each other. We have provided support and fought, but we always come back to our mutual deep love and appreciation. Now, we agree a lot more than we disagree – even on politics.

Seeing marriage and parenthood through first meant navigating our own families. Andrew grew up in Montreal, Canada and came out when he was fifteen. By the time he met Karim, his sexuality was not an issue for his immediate family, though, like many queer people, especially queer Arabs, Andrew's coming out was not straightforward.

One of our hurdles was the inter-familial closeness between our respective families, especially since the wider community and extended family did not know about our sexuality. During the early days of chatting online, we found out that Andrew's mum and Karim's father both came from Marjeyoun, and there was also a direct family tie: Andrew's great aunt had married Karim's grandmother's cousin. Andrew had mentioned attending a great uncle's funeral when Karim made the connection. The initial shock wore off quickly once we realised the connection was one of marriage and not a blood relation.

The closeness between our families has proven to be a great benefit. It has allowed our mums, despite the distance between Lebanon and Canada and the fact they have never met in person, to connect. They chat remotely during holidays, birthdays and on other occasions, without necessarily centring our relationship. When Karim's brother visited Montreal last Christmas, Andrew's mother received him with the warmth reserved for family, serving him the coffee and Christmas sweets he hadn't been able to share with family since his last visit to Beirut, four years before. When Andrew's mum visits us in London, she visits Karim's cousins. The shared Marjeyoun heritage provides a lot of conversation material, including around food, though the family recipes that have been passed down differ slightly and these kitchen squabbles can get quite heated …

Without ever telling Andrew's Sitto Wadia and Jiddo Romeo that we were together, Karim's relationship to Marjeyoun facilitated an instant connection with them, especially to Sitto Wadia. The first time Sitto met Karim, on finding out his last name, she discovered he was related to a Dr Chedid, who, back in 1940s Marjeyoun, had misdiagnosed Sitto's late sister. It was a decades-old vendetta. Andrew's mum, mortified, knew where the story was headed and thankfully interrupted his Sitto's attack on Karim. Whenever they saw one another after that, Sitto would sit for hours and tell Karim stories of the characters in the village, connecting with her hometown in ways she wasn't otherwise able to, since her age made travel to Lebanon impossible.

Conventions around 'coming out' go out the window if you are a queer Arab. We had been living together for about a year and a half when Karim's mum, on a trip to London, asked him whether Andrew was a friend or a *friend*. Not wanting to lie, Karim told her that we were together. The initial shock was difficult to swallow but she eventually realised that her love for her son, and the love that Karim and Andrew shared together, was more important than meeting any social norms or expectations. Now, Karim's mum often shares gossip with Andrew, referring to him as her third son on more than one occasion. Andrew enjoys the complaints and characters, often turning the gossip into jokes. On one occasion, a family member married at short notice. When Karim's mum complained about the timing, Andrew joked that perhaps a baby was on the way. Though the bride wasn't pregnant, it gave Karim's mum and Andrew something to look for and share inside jokes about during the wedding.

When it comes to our own relationship, we have never hidden anything. Karim's parents have stayed in our London home on numerous occasions and we visit Lebanon once or twice a year, where Karim's parents host us. Yet Karim's father has sought to remain relatively ignorant on the specifics of our relationship and we have never felt the urgency to explicitly address it with him. This does not mean he doesn't acknowledge us as a couple or a family, he does – he just doesn't say it. He still welcomes Andrew and includes him, as do Karim's brother and extended family of cousins, uncles and aunts. But what's the point of putting a label on something that he may not understand? While we attempt to emulate a heteronormative family model – something we can probably be accused of, having been married for nearly ten years and being at the start of an adoption process – much of our understanding of love, care and family has come from our experience navigating our sexualities as Arabs in the diaspora and in Lebanon. Our families handle our relationship in a manner that feels comfortable to them and respects the two of us.

The relative ease with which our families have accepted our relationship means that the additional pressures that we would otherwise face when considering children have been alleviated, creating space for us to focus on one another and on our future – though it has taken a decade for all of us to become ready for the next step.

When we reached the position, professionally and personally, where we felt that we could grow our family, we began to have more serious discussions about what that might look like. For Andrew, the economic market of surrogacy, where women are paid to offer their bodies for others, is entangled in a patriarchal system. While women have autonomy to offer their bodies as vessels to produce more babies, they are often not legally permitted to use their bodies for sex work and can be criminalised for doing so. The support for surrogacy also stands in contrast to the limitations on women's reproductive choices, including difficulties for women in accessing safe abortion in many parts of the world. Andrew has consistently questioned how surrogacy, which allows women to put great strain on their bodies and mental health, provides very little aftercare to women, especially if a woman experiences post-partum depression and bodily disassociation. Although it's assumed that women offer their bodies out of their own free will, the limitations on bodily autonomy elsewhere underscores a politics he does not want to be part of. Gay men of certain privilege often see surrogacy as a route to build families, but this can reduce women to baby-making machines and contribute towards existing forms of misogyny within the gay-male community. So for Andrew, adoption was the obvious way to start a family.

For Karim, the journey to adoption was more difficult. A significant breakthrough came when our social worker recommended us a book, *No Matter What: An Adoptive Family's Story of Hope, Love and Healing* by Sally Donovan, an uplifting true story about a straight white English couple who can't conceive and go through adoption instead. When reading it, Karim found the words for the grief he feels at the thought of not having biological children. Reading the words of this woman, whose experience was so different from his own, he could relate to that grief and felt able to articulate his own.

Karim thought he had shed that grief as he came to terms with his sexuality, but grieving takes time. It hits you when you least expect it and in unexpected places. Karim does not have nephews or nieces and he still carries the guilt of 'choosing' to stop his nuclear family's legacy. But as he learned more about adoption, he was able to process the grief and guilt. Eventually, Karim saw his path to parenthood – our path to parenthood – through adoption.

Andrew had a feeling Karim would come around to adoption once he dealt with the questions of genes and legacy. The realisation for Karim that this was not such an important issue, that what he craved was providing a caring and loving home where a child could thrive, meant that together we could move forward in the journey of starting a family. It was an exciting moment for both of us.

People outside our families have one of two responses when we tell them we are in the adoption process.

The first response is overly enthusiastic, making out that we are heroes in some way. Being put on a pedestal is deeply uncomfortable. We are not adopting to be celebrated, we are adopting because we want to start a family and adoption is our best option.

Others respond by telling us how adopted kids turn out – if we may speak in hyperbole – to become violent drug addicts and that it is always better to have biological children. This is also unhelpful. Proclamations of failure before we have even had a chance to build our family are incredibly defeatist. What this really does is put doubts in our own minds about the kind of love and care those individuals can show our future child.

We know that an adopted child may come to us with a mountain of trauma and attachment issues. We know the parenting we will have to engage in must be therapeutic and specific to the history and needs of the child. We know that adoption is the more difficult choice. We know that the adoption process is invasive, not just in terms of attending training and information sessions – something biological parents don't really have to do – but also because a social worker will explore every minute detail of our lives, from our families and friends to our traumas, and literally into every nook and cranny of our home. The invasive nature of the adoption process is to ensure that the adoption will not break down, exposing the child to further trauma. Social workers need to make sure the home is suitable, that the dynamic between the adopting parents is healthy and that their own histories won't be a cause for concern. For those of us who want to centre the wellbeing of a child who comes into our home, these checks are also a validating process.

When we settled on adoption to expand our family, we explored both international and domestic routes. We considered adopting from Lebanon. In many Arab and Muslim countries, adoption is not legally possible due to Islamic principles that emphasise the importance of biological lineage. Instead, a *kafala* system exists where orphaned children can be cared for, but without the legal relationship. However in Lebanon, where there are also significant Christian and Druze populations, adoption follows the law of the religious community that the adopting parents belong to. While gay marriage – or gay relationships more generally – is and are not recognised in Lebanon, Karim, as a Lebanese citizen, explored adopting through the Catholic church as a single man. This route is legally permissible, but the barriers were still too high. The church rules dictate that the adopting parent needs to be single, at least forty-two years old and can produce proof that they are not biologically able to have children. Karim would need to wait another five years before he could adopt and would then need to apply for international adoption to bring the child home to London, where the child could finally be registered as having two parents.

We began to explore domestic adoption in the UK in 2020. We contacted a charity that friends had used to adopt their son. While they had an overall positive experience, the charity's social and cultural expectations were too rigid for us. They insisted that Karim must come out explicitly to his father. They could not accept the relationship as it was and even asked Karim to sever his relationship with his father if he could not come out to him. Of course we will have to have a conversation with Karim's father – we will have to tell both Karim's parents that we will be having a child together in the next year or two. But that conversation will happen on Karim's terms as we progress, not on the terms of a charity that doesn't understand our cultural nuances.

Closing the door to the charity was difficult but we found a better home with the local council. All sorts of families seem to pass through the council and the large increase of LGBTQ+ couples going through the process meant we didn't feel the need to go through a tailored same-sex specific process. The lack of a LGBTQ+ process actually made us more comfortable in our discussions with council social workers. Andrew felt that the defined LGBTQ+ process or programme was based on Western conceptions of LGBTQ+ life and norms. Dealing with the council, and without the LGBTQ+ focus, our sexuality felt less fetishised. More care was placed on cultural and intersectional concerns.

Progressing with the council was straightforward. We were asked to read two books, do some further research and volunteer with children. Karim already had experience volunteering with children as a pen-pal and a reader. He decided to volunteer with a children's play organisation as well. Andrew began volunteering as a reader at an elementary school around the corner from our home.

About six months later, we attended our first Foundation Training session, an opportunity to learn more about adoption and a chance to meet other couples at the same stage of the process. This is considered the first big step in the adoption process. Of the four couples present, three were same sex, but we were the only non-white same-sex couple.

The social workers running the training expressed the benefit of matching with a child who shared a heritage and racial background with the adoptive parents. The training session emphasised the importance of culture, which the adoptive parents and the child can bond over. Many of the children who are looking for homes in London, where we live, are of mixed racial heritage. The council want to make sure that adoptive parents are attuned to the importance of heritage and that prospective parents will allow their child to explore their ancestry and give them the tools they need to engage with their cultures. That made sense.

We have always made an effort to understand the complexities of our own heritage and family dynamics. Even within the strictures of biological family units, understanding family histories and heritage has not been easy for us. Growing up in the diaspora, Andrew always found it important to maintain the cultural traditions of his grandparents. Throughout his childhood he was keen to learn about where his grandparents came from and why they left. Although there was never shame around Andrew's family history, aspects of it were fragmented. It was only when Andrew's mum found birth certificates for his great grandparents that a complete picture began to take form. His grandfather's parents were originally from the Syrian Golan Heights, a village named Jubbata ez-Zeit which was ethnically cleansed in the 1967 Six-Day War. An Israeli ski resort, Neve Ativ, now sits on top of the village. Not all his questions could be answered, so Andrew turned to academic studies of the history and politics of the Middle East and North Africa.

Karim's interest began through conversations with his Téta from an early age. Though he never met his grandfather, Karim's aunt found his late grandfather's papers documenting his birth home in Haifa and his work and national IDs. This discovery deepened Karim's interest in his family's Palestinian history. But when he began researching, he faced a lot of resistance from the older generation in his family. It seemed in part that they were ashamed to be associated with the dispossession and forced expulsion of the Nakba and the stigma attached to it in Lebanese society. They also wanted to protect themselves from the trauma and were guarding the history accordingly.

Discovering these histories has allowed each of us to better understand how we came to exist, if not who we are.

While every effort is made to match a child with adoptive parents who have at least some familiarity with the child's heritage, sometimes it is not possible. In our part of London, children of mixed Greek and Turkish heritage are more likely to need adopting. It is less common for children of Arab ancestry to come into the system. This has to do with the socio-economic factors of this demographic, along with waves of Arab immigration. We don't doubt that we will love any child that we connect with and who comes into our home – we understand family not through homogeneity, but as supporting individuality and nurturing diversity – but we also quickly realised that it would mean a lot to us to adopt a child with some Middle Eastern heritage, so that we could explore that together with them.

Our responsibilities as adoptive immigrant parents differ from birth parents. We will need to search for connections with our child. Our future child may not have a strong sense of biological histories of their own. Boxes of documents may not be waiting in the corner of a closet, but we can still build a general picture together of where they come from and participate in cultural practices with them. This will allow a child to connect with their own heritage and provides an opportunity for us to be part of their heritage, reaffirming the family as a unit.

Providing the opportunities for a child to explore who they are and how they belong to the world is so important. We hope that we will be able to fill whatever gaps exist for our future child by providing a stable foundation and a set of traditions that are uniquely ours. For us, this is what home is, somewhere where care, support and love are abundant. Home is a stepping stone to explore the world for a child. For us, providing for a child will make our already-full home complete.

It is still early days for us in the adoption journey – we are looking at a year to a-year-and-a-half timeline until we can be matched with a child who will join our home. But we've been thinking about how our child will refer to us: Karim will be Baba and Andrew, Daddy. Our child will have two Tétas, one Jiddo and one Papou. Using these titles reflects Karim's native Arabic and Andrew's native English as well as the heritage of our child's Lebanese and Greek grandparents. We imagine that our parents will take part in our family life, learning about the culture and heritage of our child. We will be able to celebrate diversity within a family unit and nurture belonging across the generations.

We are also starting to imagine how the physical spaces of our home may transform. We are already considering the kinds of family dynamics we would like to develop. We would like to create a play area in the family room and decorate the bedroom upstairs. We know the layout of the garden where – without a doubt – our child will play football and dig up worms, will change.

Then, of course, there is the kitchen. Food has always been a big part of building our home together. Rediscovering old family recipes and arguing over the right way to make certain dishes has become one of our traditions, especially when it comes to recipes that come from the respective Marjeyouni branches of our families. We have also added our own twists on things, like Karim's *kish'k manakeech* and Andrew's pancakes with *debs el kharroub* and pistachios. We also regularly cook hybrid dishes from other cultures, such as Turkish or Armenian eggs, *putanesca* pastas and *za'atar* focaccia. There is plenty of room to add more recipes to the mix.

We often discuss how our routines will change and the

challenges we may face. There is much to do and things that we will just have to work out together, as we go along. But more than anything, we are looking forward to caring for our future child, exploring the world with them and building our little family beyond our beloved Othello. We can only hope that Othello, who continues to demand much of our attention, will acclimatise to a new addition.

ALISSAR GAZAL

CLUB ARAK: TWENTY-THREE YEARS OF PARTYING, POLITICS AND PROTEST

I never envisaged that I would be running a successful dance party in my mid-sixties.

I began Club Arak in my forties. It was January 2002 and I had just buried my mother, who I had been nursing for several years. My father died in 1997 and after his death, my mother became my focus. Although I felt guilty admitting it, I felt a deep sense of liberation after my parents' deaths. I was no longer answerable to my immediate family; my freedoms had been unshackled from my *wajbate* (duty). But my feelings were conflicted, for though I was free, I also felt bereft and lost. I needed a break, so my partner Barbara and I left Sydney and went to visit friends in London.

It was an affirming trip in many ways. I left part of my old self behind in Sydney, but Barbara and I also spent the trip catching up with old London friends. During the visit, we were invited to a Bhangra music party. It was a sea of South Asians in magnificent outfits – men in saris, butches in khamis. I danced for three hours nonstop to a mix of Bollywood-inspired music that incorporated disco, folk, pop, soul and some Arabic dance grooves, too. The signs on the wall set the tone: 'this is a safe place', they said, and it was. 'Why don't we do this in Sydney?' I asked myself.

A *hafla* (party) is always a great opportunity to gather and meet people. But as queer Arabs, going to a more formal, sometimes stuffy *hafla* with parents and other family members, whether it be a wedding reception or a community party in a local hall, was done out of *wajbate* rather than desire. Dancing with Barbara was always done at a distance. While we were stuck in a room full of straight Arabs celebrating their straight lives and all the privileges that came with it, our physical contact was subtle and limited.

Meanwhile, my dear friend Foufu held *haflas* at her place on a regular basis, where our circle of queer Arab friends and acquaintances gathered to smoke, laugh, talk, pick up but mostly, to dance. Dancing at these parties to our music, expressing ourselves in a safe and familiar place, was therapeutic. We danced like we couldn't dance at our siblings' and cousins' weddings. We danced alone and in the centre of the room, where we were watched and admired, or we danced up close and personal with someone special – or soon to be special.

Many of us did go to established gay clubs up and down Oxford Street, Sydney's famous queer precinct. But dancing to *doff doff doff doff* music didn't suit our bodies or our minds. It certainly didn't suit me. I didn't like the music at those venues, nor did I like the vibe. I felt that something was missing but I couldn't put my finger on it. But when I danced at Foufu's *haflas* I felt elated, freed, unshackled from constraints. This was largely to do with the fact that we only played the latest and the best of Arabic music at her parties and while doing so, we all ripped the dancefloor.

On my return from London, I caught up with Foufu and proposed the idea of a public Arabic dance party that doubled as a safe space for queers of all colours. She was all for it. We named it Club Arak, a play on the Arabic word *arak*, which refers to both the aniseed-flavoured alcoholic drink from the Levant that turns milky white when mixed with water, and sweat. Hence our motto: 'prepare to sweat'.

After choosing a venue and settling on a first date that November, we began to publicise the event. As social media was virtually non-existent at the time, we relied heavily on word-of-mouth hype. We had little to no budget, so we armed ourselves with business cards with the Club Arak logo on one side and the party details on the other. We attended as many queer events as we possibly could. We also walked the streets of Sydney where the community hung out, handing out cards to anyone that looked Arab, Mediterranean or any other person of colour. We may have discriminated, but we didn't care – we were determined to make it a safe space for our community. The Gay Games were being held in Sydney at the time and the atmosphere was carnival-like, thanks to the many athletes and sports fans visiting from overseas and interstate. Our first party was held soon after the Gay Games: 22 November 2002. By the time the day came around, we had sold out all 350 tickets.

On the night of the party, a friend came to the box office and beckoned me and Foufu out onto the street, where there was a massive line of people waiting to get in. I couldn't believe it. It was such a diverse crowd. Although Club Arak is a queer Arab dance party, it resonated with the wider queer community from the beginning – Turkish, Iranian, Greek, Balkan, Italian, African, Asian, Desi, Anglo-Irish and partygoers from other ethnicities all came to support us. That November, Club Arak was born.

From a one-off party, Club Arak grew to three nights a year. We used different venues for our early events before settling upon Manning Bar at the University of Sydney, which became Club Arak's home until 2009. We kept our publicity low-key and relied on word of mouth to spread the word. By our third event we were already attracting 800–900 partygoers each night. Local queer media, like *Lesbians on the Loose* and *Star Observer,* always sent photographers to the parties and wrote up features afterwards, which they printed alongside photos of hot, beautiful people. In 2003, Club Arak was nominated for the most influential LGBTQI community event at the Sydney Star Observer Pride Week Awards. We lost out to the organisers of the Gay Games, but the nomination helped to cement our standing.

For the first seven years DJ Gemma, a popular, established Sydney DJ, played at each party. Although Gemma had a Levantine background, she had not played exclusively Arabic music at parties before. At first, she was quite nervous about whether such events could be successful. For those first few years, Foufu and I spent many hours with Gemma listening to the latest Arabic dance grooves or passing on CDs that we acquired on our many trips back and forth to Lebanon. By the end of 2009 we noticed that Gemma's music was shifting to more 'tribal' than Arabic and our regular crowd had stopped coming to our parties. It was becoming obvious to Foufu and I that we needed to make changes. We wanted a more flexible DJ who could keep up with the changing music scene and who could meet the needs of our most supportive partygoers. It became difficult for us to maintain an ongoing relationship with DJ Gemma, so we parted ways. She will always be credited for her important role in making Club Arak successful.

In 2011, after a two-year hiatus, we made a comeback with DJ Chadi spinning the tunes. He had just migrated to Australia and was already known in some circles as one of the most popular DJs in Beirut, where he used to play at Club Acid. Having him DJing with us at Club Arak was a huge win; he helped bring back the old crowd as well as draw in new partygoers. Chadi was our resident DJ for fourteen years, only stepping aside in 2025 when he moved to Melbourne. While he will always be part of the Club Arak family, we also saw this as an opportunity to invite emerging local Arab Australian DJs to play, giving them a platform and a space to explore and enhance their talent.

At the same time as Club Arak was making its comeback, Foufu and I became busier, with increased demands from our jobs and personal lives. Hosting three parties a year was too much for us, so we scaled back to two: one in the month leading up to the Sydney Mardi Gras Parade, one of the largest Pride festivals in the world, and the other in the second half of the year. We went back to roving venues, taking Club Arak to the Factory Theatre in Marrickville, Upstairs Midnight Shift (now Universal) and Kinselas Hotel – two venues in or just off Oxford Street – and downstairs at The Imperial Erskineville, an iconic venue that had a starring role in the classic Australian film *The Adventures of Priscilla, Queen of the Desert*. We always sought venues that had an outdoor balcony. The balcony became an essential element of our parties; it's where people met, caught up, chatted and discussed anything and everything over a few drinks and some cigarettes. The atmosphere on the balconies captured the essence of our original salon parties, which we ran before the big parties took off, on the odd Sunday afternoon, at a jazz bar. These Salons were relaxed gatherings with friends, family and children, with chilled Arabic tunes playing in the background. The Salons also featured live music and other performances, such as spoken-word poetry. Club Arak wasn't always about partying. Low-key community gatherings were just as important to us.

Alongside this feeling of community, some things have stayed the same throughout all these years of Club Arak parties. The midnight show is one of them. At every club night, a variety of performers, from belly dancers to interpretive dancers, political satirists to live musicians, take to the stage at midnight for a live performance. At first, the performers were just me and Foufu and our friends, but by the third event, people were approaching us requesting to perform. I had almost a decade of theatrical experience and we insisted on maintaining artistic and theatrical integrity at every midnight show. Sometimes we met with interested parties to discuss and workshop their ideas. Sometimes we stumbled on performers when we saw them live and decided they suited our event. But many were original, created by us. In our research for performance ideas, we came across numerous images via the Arab Image Foundation of people cross dressing and same-sex couples kissing. We printed and displayed them on the walls for everyone to see as they entered the party: a poignant reminder that we have always existed.

In 2023, Sydney was chosen as the host city for World Pride and Club Arak was invited to hold a party at Kinselas. With thousands of overseas visitors descending for the week, the city was buzzing. This was never going to be a regular Club Arak party. We were given access to three floors, one of which had a balcony overlooking the fiesta taking place on the streets below. With more than 970 tickets sold online and 200 at the door, over a thousand people attended the event. It was our biggest party yet. We threw every iconic element of our gay and lesbian lives on the stage and dance floor. We invited Clarissa Bitar to perform – a young Palestinian oud player who resides in LA. The honeyed voice of our local talent, Hussein Kahill (and his Iraqi band) also delighted the crowds. The *pièce de résistance* was the midnight show featuring The Three Divas, a performance trio consisting of myself, Hussein Kahill and Paula, a friend and Club Arak regular. Our act paid homage to the three major Arab divas: Umm Kulthum, Fairuz and Sabah. We rehearsed for weeks and organised the best outfits, from dresses to shoes to wigs, make-up and jewellery. Our entrance onto the stage sent the crowd into a frenzy. It was joyful and heartwarming – most people knew the words and sang along as loudly as they could. Their voices resonated throughout the venue, reminding us all that although the songs were forty, fifty or even sixty years old, they had crossed generations.

Although social and religious constraints have rejected and denied our existence throughout history, we have always found a way to express our existence with flair and pride. One of these ways is through honouring our deeply loved icons. Umm Kulthum has the whole Arab world swooning at her songs. She married late and it's a common rumour that this was a marriage of convenience, especially since she had no children. This may not mean anything, but we still all see her as our Arab lesbian icon. Fairuz is a quintessential Lebanese diva. Her songs speak to the diaspora of tradition, identity, love and the agony of missing the smell and feel of the homeland that gave us life and our culture. Meanwhile, Sabah was a star. Her hair, make-up and glamour made her beloved by gay men and drag queens everywhere. The legacy of Umm Kulthum, Fairuz and Sabah in Arab culture and music is immense and inspires performers to this day. Some of those who have paid tribute to them include Bassem Feghali, a Lebanese drag queen, who has gained fame for his impersonations of Sabah and other contemporary divas like Haifa Wehbe and Nancy Ajram. One of our most popular midnight show acts was by mine and Foufu's friend Brett, who impersonated Haifa Wehbe at Club Arak. Wearing the most exquisite red dress, Brett walked through 800 screaming people to reach the stage.

As well as being great fun, our midnight shows often carried strong political and social messages that exposed issues facing not just Arab queers, but Arab Australians as well. One of our most satirical shows was in response to the second Gulf War and the so-called 'Axis of Evil'. Three warrior performers, Mina, Zeina and Deina (also known as 'The Waxers of Evil') destroyed George W. Bush and Australia's then Prime Minister John Howard on stage, under the direction of a butch aunty. Their weapons included karate kicks, the evil eye and the humble shoe, which they threw at the warlords' faces.

Regardless of the tone of the midnight shows, we have always believed that the entire existence of Club Arak was in itself a political statement. Our existence as queer Arabs, our right to self-expression, joy and determination to be seen and heard has always been our focus. When the political climate demeaned us or our families, in the diaspora or in the homeland, we kicked back and we did it with style. We have never shied away from politics. We have always made fierce statements while maintaining a safe space for queer Arabs to make friends, meet lovers and nurture one another. Club Arak has become more than just a dance party: it is a conduit for many, a bridge that brings private lives out from the closet and into a public space.

Our most cherished comments come from partygoers who are not out to their families. They love their parents and are loved back, but as one partygoer once told me, 'I don't want to break their hearts, that would kill me.' These people also love to dance at *haflas* with their family and friends, but are torn that they can't take their *habibti* (darling) with them. It is for them that Club Arak still exists.

Keeping our sexuality a secret from family is almost a full-time job. It requires a lot of phone calls – at least it did before the rise of social media and smartphones. Seeing each other was easy, as our parents were content that we were hanging out with other Arab friends, but, like most of my Arab friends, our social lives took place in private rather than in public. Our gatherings always started with a barbecue at a friend's place that went on until the early hours of the morning. If we were in a public space, we would go far enough away from the suburbs where our parents and relatives lived that no one we knew would see us. While information about what was happening in the Sydney queer scene was available in magazines, we had to make sure that we got rid of them, especially if we still lived with family.

Our families – especially our parents – came first. The love we have for our parents was greater than our need for self-liberation. Many of my queer Arab friends lived in the western suburbs of Sydney either with, or near, their families. The parents of those who lived in the inner west or inner city, away from the Arab community hubs of the west, maintained a vigilant watch over their children's movements. When it came to maintaining our closeted lives, we didn't have to explain to each other why we were doing it. Most of us understood and supported each other. Club Arak parties, alongside the *haflas* we had in our homes and salons, were not just a welcome change from the humdrum of our double existence – they were our saviour.

When Barbara and I began our relationship in 1993, both my parents were still alive. Coming out to them was not an option. To many people in the queer community that decision does not make sense. For them, coming out and being free of social constrains is part of our liberation journey. But if you are a migrant from the Global South or the child of such migrants, that is not usually our journey. In a western country like Australia, we carry the responsibility of our parents' sacrifice to give us a better life on our shoulders and in our hearts. Being out is a privilege only white people have. White Australians have the privilege of their skin colour and of belonging from birth. As a person of colour – and even after fifty-two years in Australia – the privilege of belonging is not afforded to me.

My premier identity is not my sexuality. It is, in order, my gender, ethnicity and skin colour and *then* my sexuality. Coming out was never a priority when I had so many other facets of my identity to tackle.

Nonetheless, it took over ten years for my siblings and other family members to come to terms with my sexuality and my partner. Our relationship is now nearing thirty-two years and Barbara is my anchor, compass and an integral part of the family. My nephew, nieces and grandnephews see her as an aunty.

Barbara and I met in front of Sydney Town Hall in 1991 protesting at an anti-Gulf War rally. I was standing among many Arab friends and she was standing with her Jewish colleagues under a banner that read 'Jewish Women for an Independent Palestine'. That blew me away. I didn't know that Jews like that existed. I walked up to the group and started a conversation, which resulted in Barbara's group and numerous Arab women, myself included, gathering to plan political activities. Barbara had just come back from London, where she and a group of Jewish women had established a local branch of 'Women in Black', a pro-Palestine, anti-Israeli occupation movement that began in Israel in 1987. The women used to meet every week and hold silent vigils in all the major cities in Israel, wearing black, carrying placards. In Israel it was mostly Jewish women, but in London and then Sydney and Melbourne, it was cross-cultural.

Although Barbara and I had known and worked with each other for two years, our romance did not start until late 1993. Not long after that (in the great lesbian tradition) Barbara moved in. Our relationship has since lasted longer than the Oslo Accords and countless ceasefire agreements. Our political activism is central to our relationship. Since the start of the genocide on Palestinians in Gaza, we have both remained vigilant and continue our solidarity with Palestinians, Lebanese and Syrians suffering under the colonialist yoke.

It is impossible sometimes to separate a personal and professional life, just as it is impossible to isolate one idea of home from another. Living and loving in Sydney, there was always a hidden reminder that I didn't belong. Sometimes I felt a thirst for a replenishment from the homeland. I migrated from Lebanon with my family in my mid teens, but I still felt the need to visit regularly. What I witnessed on these visits informed what we programmed and how we ran Club Arak.

Lebanon has always prided itself on being a modern and

open society. Although we have sectarian, religious and political constraints, the Lebanese themselves are contradictory in their modern social outlook.

To some extent, running a party night in Sydney caught some of the underground feel of queer parties in Lebanon. After the end of the civil war in 1990, the Lebanese queer community established many underground parties and gatherings, although supportive organisations were not established until the 2000s. Helem, established in 2000, was the first queer rights organisation in the Arab world. Meem, a lesbian, bisexual, trans and queer women's group, followed in 2007. In that year, on one of my visits to Lebanon, I had the opportunity to meet the young Philosophy PhD candidate who established Meem. She invited me to a meeting at a yoga centre in Beirut's Hamra district. Many of the fifteen women showed up with yoga mats to maintain the façade, as the gathering took place on a weekend and the doorman was inquisitive. While the others shared their stories, frustrations and tribulations with each other, as a visitor I kept quiet for the duration of the meeting. All the time I kept thinking that I needed to make a documentary about the lesbians of Lebanon. So, I did.

Over three weeks, I met and interviewed those who were willing to participate. The result was a twenty-minute documentary called *Lesbanese*. The documentary was first screened privately in 2009 at the Meem offices. It was never screened publicly in Lebanon to protect the participants' safety, but it was seen at many film festivals worldwide, including queer film festivals in Sydney and Melbourne, and won best short documentary at the Toledo Film Festival in the US.

Meanwhile, the nightclub scene in Beirut in the 90s and early 2000s was fantastic. Dancing and clubbing in the Lebanese capital has always been brilliant but the queer dance parties were really something quite special. Between 1998 and 2001, Club Acid and B 018 were the places to be. The music and the vibe were unparalleled and they both influenced Club Arak in many ways. Club Acid was hugely popular yet remained a bit of a secret, until it was closed down by local political entities. Many other clubs have come and gone or have survived and thrived. Today, Beirut has many nightclubs and bars that cater to a wide clientele without necessarily advertising their queerness. Their popularity and ability to change and shift with the times is inspiring.

The Lebanese are the ultimate capitalists. Making money is an important part of their existence. Although many of the bars are straight, on the odd occasion they have a special queer night arranged by word of mouth only. The owners turn a blind eye: business is business. On one of my visits, we heard about a queer dance party at a popular nightclub and asked a taxi driver to take us there. We spent fifteen minutes in the taxi arguing with him. He was adamant that the bar was closed on Wednesday nights, but we knew better. When we arrived, he was shocked to see that it was open and that there were many people outside trying to get in. Of course, we didn't tell him it was queer dance night.

We all have memories of being on the outside, of trying to get in. Of trying to become part of something that has meaning. Of wanting to be somewhere we feel we belong and where we are comfortable with who we are. I still remember our second Club Arak party, which also sold out. The flip side to that was that sadly, there were many people waiting outside who couldn't get in. We had surpassed the venue's capacity and had to shut the doors. I was the door bitch as usual and needed to escape the heat, so I went outside for some fresh air. I saw a tall, shy man standing by the door, hoping to gain entry. We started a conversation. He was a recently arrived migrant from Bangladesh, currently living in the western suburb of Lakemba in a strict Muslim household. He was desperate to be at a party like Club Arak. We talked, we laughed, we hugged and I sneaked him in. After that, he came to every event, always showing up early so he did not miss out on a ticket.

So many queer Arabs have reached out over the years to tell us that we helped change their lives by simply hosting a party. Many felt confident and empowered as a result of spending time in that environment. One of our regulars felt so confident that he invited his mother to attend one of our parties with him. She came and danced with us all, we felt so elated when we saw her – it was like all our mothers were there. Another friend, who had married and had two children in an effort to hide his homosexuality, eventually left his family to pursue his own life. When his son came out to him, their way of celebrating was to come to Club Arak together. A cousin of mine invited a young Melkite priest to our first party, who danced all night and came out a few years later. He never stopped coming to our events, but he did stop being a priest.

When we held our hugely successful World Pride party in 2023, it was admittedly hard to stop and catch up with anyone. But I did spot a woman that I had not seen for over ten years. She used to be a regular at our events and had performed as one of the dancers in our midnight shows. I headed over to her for a quick chat and she introduced me to a gorgeous young man who turned out to be her eighteen-year-old son. He had always wanted to come to Club Arak, so they came to celebrate their queerness together. It gives me much pleasure to know that this *hafla* is medicine not only for me and Foufu, but to the Club Arak family and now, after twenty-two years, to their children too.

The popularity of Club Arak helped empower others to establish their own events. One of our most ardent fans and a regular midnight show performer established Beit El Hob (House of Love). For several years, on the first Wednesday of every month, Beit El Hob gatherings took place at a popular gay pub where we met, talked, drank and supported one another. Some brought their parents or siblings along. Discussions often veered into politics and heated debates. Many of us didn't want to be political, especially newly arrived migrants, but others had strong opinions and many were politically active. Disagreements were inevitable and that's okay – we are not a homogenous group. It is more important to be able to express our views in a safe space.

There is now a proliferation of Arab dance parties in Melbourne and Sydney headed by numerous DJs who identify strongly with their Arab heritage and influence. But back when Club Arak began, our lives were divided in two. At home and in the car we blasted our Arabic music, singing along or simply listening, depending on the context. We mostly kept that music to ourselves. When we had gatherings that included non-Arab friends, we listened to other popular music. We were interested in Western music, but Arabic music was personal, emotional and grounding. We valued the connection to our culture it provided. Twenty-two years later, my friends and I don't shy away from playing our Arab music playlists at mixed gatherings. It is now the expected thing and many non-Arab friends even request it for their parties.

Though our music felt underground, Arab culture in Sydney and Melbourne maintained its influence in the culinary corner: Lebanese restaurants are everywhere and on weekends there is always a bad belly dancer swaying in front of white men and getting them to dance with her. Although we hated witnessing that, we loved the music and the food and especially the private cushion rooms where we could have intimate gatherings for friends' birthdays or other special occasions. But away from the culinary and foodie hubs, Arab culture in general in Australia was misunderstood and misrepresented. While everyone wanted to visit our restaurants or learn how to make hummus, everything else was feared or fetishised. Racism and discrimination was, and still is, rife.

In 2005 the Cronulla riots rocked Sydney and grabbed headlines nationwide. White men – riding the post-9/11 anti-Arab and Islamophobia wave – roamed the streets of Cronulla and its world-famous beach to attack anyone who looked

Middle Eastern with cricket bats, sticks and fists in broad daylight. Cronulla Beach is in the heart of 'The Shire', the nickname given to the local council authority of Sutherland Shire that dominates Sydney's southern suburbs, and is a predominantly white, affluent and conservative-leaning area. But it's also close to the southwestern suburbs of Sydney, a predominantly working class, multicultural area where many Arab families live. Prime Minister John Howard insisted that Australia did not have a racism issue and that the riots were primarily a law-and-order issue. Club Arak responded with a midnight show that critiqued Australian beach culture. It finished with an Indigenous man waving the Aboriginal flag to remind everyone that Australia always was and always will be Aboriginal land.

Being brazenly political has never harmed our brand. If anything, it has made us stronger.

Whenever I mention the possibility of having one last party and putting Club Arak to bed, Foufu shuts down the conversation. As far as she is concerned Club Arak is a community service and we can't stop being there for people. If anything, we have inadvertently become the aunties of our queer Arab community in Sydney. But with every party, this sixty-six-year-old body feels older. It wants to be horizontal after midnight, not upright, dancing. Yet this twenty-three-year (and counting) journey has taught me so much about myself. It has also exposed me to the resilience and strengths of the queer Arab family. I have had the pleasure of meeting the most wonderful, loving and inspiring people of all ages; people who have been – or are currently going – through hell. I have heard harrowing stories alongside stories of love, acceptance and joy. I have been humbled by the experience and enveloped by so much gratitude and love. I will forever be grateful to Foufu who understood and shared the vision and to the love of my life, Barbara, for dancing without me all these years because I am too busy running the show.

All I ever wanted was a space to dance to my favourite music. I got so much more.

MELHEM HASAN

FROM A WINDOWLESS ROOM IN MECCA

Come round three or four, her arms were tangled in mine as the tightening crowd ebbed and flowed in circles around the Kaaba, the greatest Muslim monument in existence. Everyone is trying to complete seven rounds of *tawaf,* the act of circumambulating the Kaaba. The narrowness carried in a thousand chests so close to one another is painful and dreadful and the lack of space can cause people to act out of character, even in the context of such monumental, once-in-a-lifetime worship. Altercations between two strangers like us are not uncommon, I've come to learn.

I was already on edge that day because my father refused to let me give him his pills for his Parkinson's. Instead, he insisted on picking them out of a small plastic bag my sister had organised them in, himself. One by one he picks them, though now – in this packed environment – is not the time to be in denial about the state of his motor skills. Ten years since his diagnosis and he still rage, rage, rages against the dying of the light. I wish his rage – or mine – were enough. The woman lets me go.

Growing up, a small Muslim village child quickly learns

to look at pilgrims with great regard. When pilgrims come back from Hajj, the entryways to their houses are decorated with tree branches, lanterns and flashing lights. Pilgrimage has historically been widely viewed as a high act of devotion to God. It's often seen as someone's final act, an atonement before death. It is said that Hajj is a rebirth and a cleansing of all sin, which explains why a lot of old people go, although many young people – particularly men – make the pilgrimage too.

Very few things are written on Muslim gravestones: *martyr, baby, Hajj.* Hajj is the most profound activity a Muslim can perform. I was honestly and wholeheartedly fighting to perform it, against the constant threat of not being able to complete it.

What's a guy like me doing in Hajj? *A guy like me*, as in queer. Or *a guy like me*, as in one without a Hajj permit. In all honesty, God had little to do with the trouble of it. It's people who have made my tattooed arms and my boyfriend such hindrances at the gates of Heaven.

The tour group convinced me that everything would be alright if I came to Saudi Arabia on a tourist visa instead of a Hajj permit. I thought I needed a new war, a challenge. Then, I was arrested on my first day performing Hajj, in June – the month before my father died. Nothing about it was pretty. In the back of a Saudi police car, I realised I'd got my challenge and this was the consequence.

I should never have come without a permit, I realise, as I'm sitting in the back of the police car. Hajj is a long and difficult road. To take it while feeling constantly in danger is the last thing anyone wants. 'You'll blend in with the other pilgrims,' the tour organiser had said. He wore his beard semi-long, white and with a gap of hair between his upper lip and nose. That's how you know they take religion very seriously. They always shorten the moustache, following the example of the Prophet, or so they say. He'd managed to convince us permitless pilgrims, and perhaps himself, that it would be okay, that we would not be caught without Hajj permits and that we would be able to complete all the *manasek* (rituals) of Hajj.

I had arrived in Riyadh stripped of all material attachment to this life. There, I switched terminals and took a flight to Jeddah. A guide with the tour group met me at the airport and showed me to the car that would take me to Mecca. They'd told me to dress casually and not pack any items that may give indication of my intention to perform Hajj. Hajj Issam – that was my tour organiser's name – was even excited to see my tattoos. 'No one will be able to tell,' he said, referring to me pursuing Hajj.

The car ride from Jeddah to Mecca was the final piece of evidence I needed to know that what I was doing was illegal. A large group of us pilgrims with no Hajj visas had been brought from Jeddah to Mecca by a gang I can best describe as pilgrim smugglers. By the time the taxi pulled over in front of the hotel, my head was scrambled. I'd travelled for over twelve hours for a trip that would have normally been a two-hour flight.

I'd been dreading spending ten days waiting in Mecca, to disguise the real purpose of my trip. I knew that we were most likely to get caught in the final days, before Hajj officially began. I was right: I was exiled back to Jeddah the next morning, still nine days before the date set for the permitted pilgrims to arrive, after the police caught me having coffee in front of the hotel.

I could tell it was game over the instant the police car pulled over.

The policemen who arrested me were kind – at first. Initially, I attempted to treat the situation like it was a traffic ticket I could get out of. My big puppy eyes and confused demeanour worked on one officer, but even he required papers. To him, I was a stranger who looked very strange, too strange to be in Mecca days before Hajj: gym shorts and a t-shirt, a vape and a paper cup of coffee. Tattoos all over. There was no way I'd lose these guys or that they'd let me out of their sight for long enough for me to run. There were three officers, and one of them was not a fan of the way I looked. He said I wasn't Muslim and that only heretics wore what I wore and did what I'd done to my body, referring to my tattoos.

How could an act as pure as Hajj feel like a crime? I was trying to get closer to God with my parents, who were yet to arrive. Their visas were legitimate; they'd applied in time. But for a long time, we didn't know whether it would be three of us or just myself and my mother. My father had been suffering. He had begun the year with open heart surgery, followed by complications from Parkinson's disease. His medication was adjusted in April, around Eid al Fitr. That was when we took our last family photo. But then my father was willed to attend Hajj and the three of us made it to Mecca after all. Only I had done so illegally, because it was too late at that point for me to apply for the permit.

When I became sufficiently broken by the police, too weakened to argue about going to the station, I got in the back of their car. I was behind a metal partition, in a cage. My driver had told me the previous day what happens to people who get caught trying to undertake Hajj without a permit: you get sent back to Jeddah. You can try to sneak back in again, but a second strike means a ten-year ban.

My brother was on the phone with me for the entire journey as it became increasingly obvious that this would be a rough one to wriggle out of. I said to him, 'what if God doesn't want me here?' I needed to know if I had been stopped from undertaking Hajj by God or by the authorities. I thought perhaps the hardship I was facing to do Hajj would atone for anything I had done wrong. Maybe I had to prove that I really wanted to be there and being stopped was a divine test of my devotion. My determination to return to Mecca outweighed the risk. This trip had already taken a year's worth of patience and perseverance.

Even my brother was shocked that I still wanted to do Hajj after I had been arrested.

After we had been detained at the police station, a bus took everyone who was caught that morning without a permit and dropped us off on a roadside in Jeddah. There were several restaurants and shops there, where I was able to rest and find another taxi willing to smuggle me back to Mecca.

I had to lay low on my second try and hope that when I mixed with the pilgrims who did have Hajj permits, I'd get by without trouble. But once I made it back without incident, worse thoughts hounded me as I waited down the days for Hajj season to start. Locked away in my small hotel room, I wondered if I'd ever get to see the Kaaba.

We hear horror stories about people who have done terrible things and try to atone, only to undertake Hajj and be refused a view of the Kaaba. The superstitious say that bad people can look straight at it without seeing it. I was not afraid of that, but I did fear being turned away or stopped from entering. These thoughts went round my head as I was shut in that room, with just a large console for a television that did not work attached to a mirror and a closet for company. I had plenty of time to study the closet; its dark brown wood, aged and its knobs which must have once been golden. Now, they were rusted and grey – at least those that were left, were. The closet blocked the only window in the room. Outside, air conditioning fans droned all night and all day. Their sound was muffled by the window, which was unreachable; not that I would have opened it to let the heat in, anyway.

After over a week in that same small room, lit by a single yellow light bulb, a giant bus pulled over in front of the hotel entrance one night at 2 AM. I'd been sequestered in the room for nine days, waiting for the other pilgrims to arrive so I could blend in. 'Who'd check an entire tour of two hundred?' the sheikh reasoned. I hoped to go unnoticed in a crowd of so many. I watched as passengers, in various shades of white, disembarked from the giant bus. The men wore a uniform, single colour, pure white, consisting of two towels that we call *ihram*, which also refers to the state of purity pilgrims are in. During this time of cleansing, male pilgrims refrain from hunting, cutting their hair, clipping their nails and sexual activity, among other things. The same rules apply to the women, except for the uniform – women are allowed to wear sewn clothing of any colour, though most choose to wear the same shade as the men. I think it's beautiful that everyone is wearing a version of white. From the fourth floor, the arrivals look like angels from the sky. My mother and my father are among them. A welcome committee from the Hajj and Umrah Ministry greeted them in the hotel lobby as I helped with the luggage before I had a quick catch-up with my parents in their room. Seeing them made me feel safe.

I did the first of the *manasek* – the rites and ceremonies that have to be performed in and around Mecca as part of Hajj – with my parents, the morning after they arrived. It was Umrah. The organisers make a big point of how quickly they wanted us to complete this stage – 'in and out. Stay together' – though the road leading to Al Masjid al-Haram (shortened to 'al-Haram'), the large mosque in Mecca where the Kaaba is located, is long.

You must be specific when pronouncing 'al-Haram'. If you are referring to the full name of the mosque, the second 'a' stretches, while 'haram' meaning any 'safe haven', is pronounced with a soft 'ah.' Multiple mosques are referred to as al-Haram (with a soft 'ah'). This is different from the common use of 'haram', which means forbidden.

A huge space filled with thousands precedes the entrance to Al Masjid al-Haram, where we were instructed to take our shoes off and put them in our bags. The men among us were in towels, because we're in the state of *ihram*. We were not allowed to wear socks or underwear, but the towels can be secured with safety pins. Many people undertaking Hajj were there for the second or even a fifth time – we're supposed to set the intention while we're performing Hajj to return every year. I was lucky that one of the more experienced pilgrims, Moustafa, had given me a tip. He told me to get fully naked after *wudu*, a washing ritual essential before certain acts of worship such as prayer, to spread my legs, and to apply a towel to my bottom. This, Moustafa told me, would avoid chafing.

Upon entering Al Masjid al-Haram, we were once more reminded to stay together. There is a strategy to performing this ritual quickly and without any strays: the men form a circle around the women and on we go. I was fascinated by how this is done, with both genders mixed together in such a tight space, among an increasingly large crowd. I realised how many of the practices thrown under the umbrella of religion back home are man-made. When we finally got to our destination, I realise I can see the Kaaba. God doesn't hate me, after all.

Tawaf, the act of walking seven times around the Kaaba, is followed by a prayer. The prayer is followed by vanilla and mango ice cream on a sidewalk – not religiously mandated, although highly encouraged and somewhat essential.

The post-Umrah relief would not last. The days between then and Hajj were the ones where my anxiety recorded its highest highs. Every second felt like a reminder of the possibility of losing it all. 'Hajj is Arafa,' people often say. Once you've stood on Mount Arafa, the mountain where the

Prophet performed his final sermon, you become a Hajj, for life. It cannot be taken from you and you cannot be stripped of its meaning. But you must complete one all-important bus ride and spend the day there praying and performing dua.

A sheikh from my village was going to accompany us to Mount Arafa. His name is Youssef. Like me, Youssef came here without a permit and suffered the sequestering. He sits me down two days before the Day of Arafa as I boil over the tour's shortcomings. I wasn't given a prayer mat or a Quran. I never felt treated like a Hajj, like the others with permits were. I had also overheard the way tour organisers talk about their pilgrims – 'cows', someone called them. I felt cheated; robbed of an experience that was meant to change my life for the better. I was angry. Obviously, this feeling was wrong, in the long term. But in that hotel room, in between the different stages that make up Hajj, my horrors were too consuming for reason or rationality.

I was on my third week of waiting. My white sheets were covered in my body hair, never cleaned in my near month-long stay. I begged a kind lady on the housekeeping staff for more toilet paper and she delivered some, but this was a favour, not a given. The white plastic chair was a vacation from the bed. The bed is where I consumed all the news or sometimes wrote. I left my suitcase on the left side of the bed, open, where much of what I'd packed ended up unused. To the right side of the room was the toilet, tiny, but enough. I used only one towel during those three weeks. I'd brought another one from home, but I was saving it for *wudu*.

The room tightens. My chest follows. I endlessly replay the

image of a balloon enlarging to the point of explosion before it deflates, only to flare back up again. I am yet to explode.

I did leave my room to eat, but those were careful, brief outings. As I was sitting on a white plastic chair in the hotel restaurant, listening to the sheikh on the night before the Day of Arafa, I felt panic in every pore as I imagined being turned away just before the climax of Hajj. That would be a clear sign that God didn't want me there. After all those plane, train, bus and car rides, I could still be caught on my way to Mount Arafa and denied becoming a Hajj, a thing I wanted very badly. That would be my worst nightmare.

My parents, on the other hand, were both able to commute back and forth during the period of Hajj, between the hotel, shops and the Haram. They were not in danger of being arrested, because they both had legitimate permits. At least I did not have to worry about that.

On the Day of Arafa, the permitted pilgrims were sent on a bus early in the morning, right after Fajr prayer. We, the permitless, waited for the group chat announcement before heading down. The place was crawling with police. We were told to wait in the prayer room on the ground floor, hidden behind a wall between the prayer area and the entrance of the hotel. We waited for the sign to sneak out to the bus. If I was to make it, I would meet my parents on Arafa, within the next two hours. I'd finally have my answer and it would all be over, I told myself as my hands shook and my eyes ran like rivers on the ride. Our silence was broken as a man among us performed *Talbia*: the chant about fulfilling God's call that is repeated in mosques all around the world on Arafa day and during the four days of Eid al Adha.

The sound of *Talbia* takes me back to my childhood, when Eid was anticipated as a day of great joy. I spent the surprisingly short bus ride crying and chanting along with the others. Within the hour, we saw a sign announcing 'Beginning of Arafa'. Once we crossed that threshold, we had done it. We all chanted as Mahmoud, a tour organiser, delivered a speech: 'it wasn't your wits or your smarts. It wasn't any games you played or hurdles you've successfully overcome. It was all Him. He called on you and all you did was answer.'

I will, till the end, think of arriving at Arafa as the most important moment of my life. I am too young to properly grasp the change, but I know now that we are all seeking enlightenment in some form or another. If knowing more means having more power, and the powerful are the ones with the best chances of survival, then it is our natural instinct to seek enlightenment.

Upon arriving, we were all given seats and small food packs, but as more people began to arrive, the seating became a problem. The seats were numbered according to pilgrims with permits, so there were many more people there than there were seats. A group of sheikhs began to fight in the middle of the tent very early on during the day. I grabbed a portable chair, small and foldable, and pretended not to hear. One sheikh was particularly angry. He attacked other organisers and cussed them for bringing illegals – a problem I doubt is new. These people have been bringing pilgrims here for years, so you would think that they were used to having more pilgrims than seats. And it's not like pilgrims wouldn't share; everybody was kind – most sheikhs excluded.

The sermons delivered on that day were further proof of who was there for drama. In Arafa, sheikhs from all over the world took turns on the microphone like drag queens performing for the crowds. It was all about who cried louder, who delivered the strongest monologue. The fakery drove many of the younger men outside the tents and into the heat of the desert. We were much more useful out there, bringing water and food to older people – the temperature was just as or even more suffocating inside the tents, anyway. In the afternoon, I stepped outside with my mother and we sat by the entrance to the tent, she in a wheelchair and I, on top of a freezer. People walked in and out to smoke or take breaks from the performances going on inside. There were large groups of people who broke away from what was going on at the podium to pray and perform *dua*. The sheikhs turned into clowns in my head and the tent became a circus. It was important to remember the reason we were there.

Mount Arafa was followed by Muzdalifah, an evening prayer and an optional night's sleep there, outside. At midnight we were taken back to the hotel, but we didn't arrive till Fajr prayer, five hours later.

When we arrived back at the hotel we immediately broke from the state of *ihram*. Dozens of men flooded the narrow barbershops to shave their heads clean – to break *ihram*, we must lose some of our hair. My hair fell on the blue bib and down to the white towel covering the lower half of my body. I saw my head for the first time in years and I quietly sobbed; the catharsis of rebirth, or exhaustion.

From the barbershop we undertook a ritual that involves stoning the devil. We did this multiple times over the days of Eid. *Tawaf al Ifada* is another rite that forms part of the Hajj *manasek*, and consists of another seven rounds around the Kaaba followed by *saii*, the back-and-forth walk between the Safa and Marwa hilltops. Strange as it may sound, all of this was actually fun. We were encouraged to perform *dua* in our own ways, to talk to God in whatever language or accent we know.

We got separated from my father after *saii*. He'd left his bag with me, his phone in it. After an hour or so of panicked searching, I got a call from my older sister in Lebanon who told me my father had contacted her from a taxi. He had gone back to the hotel. I was worried that he may have been helpless on his own, forgetting how quick he was, even though his body couldn't perform as quickly as his brain. He'd been doubted, dubbed an old man. We returned to the hotel to find him and held a brief celebration, surprised how easily he had managed to return to the hotel. It sounds silly, but the tour organisers worry about older people in this way. They're not used to them being able to find their way around. Even I forgot how highly educated and aware my father still was. He too was annoyed with the way he was treated – tour organisers tend to treat the pilgrims like children. My father had been an educator his entire adult life and wasn't used to being treated like a student.

Hajj ends with the Farewell *Tawaf*. Most pilgrims moved onto Medina afterwards, to pay respects to the Prophet. Medina is an hour away from Mecca by train and it is where the Prophet was laid to rest. However, I chose to return home, leaving my parents with the tour to continue to Medina. My duties were done. I had become a Hajj.

I spent my last day in Saudi with my mother in her and my father's room; she smoked and I vaped and we talked about it all. Where we were at in life and where we're going. My father had joined our village sheikh and some other friends out for a small trip and lunch. We were all very tired of the same buffet food every day, served with a virus that infected the entire hotel within one meal. My father returned just in time, before I left for the train station. I said my goodbyes without looking back; we always think we'll get another look some other time. But the next time I saw my father was in the ICU in a Medina hospital, his eyes like glass orbs, seeing things beyond all this. I'd abandoned the traditional Mecca-Medina plan and stuck to the main obligations so that I could return to work, but I ended up visiting Medina after all, when my father fell ill.

We were supposed to talk to him, to encourage him to hold on and come back. It's entertaining and reassuring, so I told him about silly things far away from what he was likely seeing. But it must have been reassuring enough for him to let go, I guess.

I lost track of all the hospital rooms and police stations. At one point, we all stood in a hallway saying goodbye to dad. It went the way it goes; just another family in the great picture of all things, our bodies levitating and soaking in the present. Here I am, here we are before the shrouded body of my father, all of us locked in a single, long and tearful embrace, permission to finally fall apart and acknowledge the circumstances. Did I just accompany my father to Hajj, his very last act? Weren't we just children coming back from school? Where did the time go? One long, long afternoon, it seems to have been. It's gone by so quickly. Six of us dozed off and only five woke up.

There is life before Arafa and life after it. There was also life before my father and life after him. In more ways than one, I saw behind the curtain that June during Hajj and I have got my answers.

Much of the magic you see on YouTube while preparing for Hajj is lost in logistics. Practical reality looks a lot less nice. It takes real grit to survive Hajj season in Mecca; physical and mental strength, patience and strong faith. A lot of walking and waiting goes into it, sometimes hunger and dehydration. Fear, even.

Words fail to record the moment of Arafa for me, but I will try. It was like nothing I ever felt about myself was true. Everything I'd ever been told, all the deficiencies and incompletions, were never there. I had been unburdened from the baggage of other men, their agendas and ideas. Life after Arafa was freer, like I knew that nothing was ever wrong with me. It was an illusion created by men; God doesn't hate me. He has called on me and I have fulfilled: *Labbayka Allahumma labbayk* (Here I am, O Allah, Here I am); a declaration of devotion and readiness.

The scale us Muslims love to bring up, the one of good and bad, is invisible. The invisible line between queerness and Islam, which it seemed impossible to venture between, was shattered for me after Arafa. The in-between? It's all misinformation, other peoples' interpretations of ancient events and texts. From the peak of a mountain I've spent my life climbing, I saw my own history. I felt it so deeply when my present was upended with my father's death. My father, who lives in every detail of the house he built for us, in every stone he laid and every tree he raised.

After my father's death, my family go back to live a life that misses something. In its place comes the reminder that forever itself happens in intervals. Our lives are too short to be significant in any major way, except they are significant for those who are immediately next to us – the ones we love. The unimportance of self parades itself in flashes, reminding us all how little we are. How poor. How deserving of sympathy and compassion.

I put on my father's jacket for the first Eid after his passing. I put my hands in the pockets, where his hands once were. When I close my eyes, I try to go back to a time when it was him in this jacket, and I think of what he'd do. The air between the olive trees still smells like him. I brush my teeth and I take the steps down to the kitchen in tears, realising I'll open the kitchen door and only one parent will be waiting. I embrace my mother. I value life.

ABU LEILA

MY MOTHER'S PRONOUNS

We have nothing

I'm in a queer Beirut house share, mushroom risotto cooking, white walls with paint peeling off, huge windows, mouldy ceilings, revolutionary posters everywhere. I'm here on a family visit and I am delighted to have found the queers. I immediately feel at ease: I have been in endless houses like this one and it always feels like home. The inhabitants of this house dress and act in the same way as queers everywhere: strange haircuts and jokes about various forms of oppression. There is crochet all over the place like there is in my grandma's house. I'm lounging on an old flower-printed sofa, chatting to a man who looks a lot like Hamed Sinno, the lead singer of Lebanese band Mashrou' Leila. He says to the room: 'I don't think gay people should have rights in the Middle East.'

I look at his arms, which are draped around his boyfriend's shoulders.

'You don't think you should have rights?'

'No.'

He takes the following silence as an opportunity to launch into a speech, swinging between Arabic and English. 'We don't have human rights here and you want us to have gay rights? My mother doesn't even know about straight sex. If you ask my mother did she ever kiss my father, she would tell you that is disgusting. We have nothing, not even a heterosexual kiss. She doesn't think it's okay for her to find my father sexy. And you want me to go tell her I love having sex with my boyfriend, who is a drag queen?'

The boyfriend smiles and sinks into the sofa.

'She would be unhappy to hear it and I would gain nothing. I am telling you: we have nothing, no electricity, no democracy, no safety, no talking about heterosexual married sex or enjoying it. The last thing we should be talking about is gay rights. If you want to be proud go to Europe. I will be secret forever.'

Mother, take one

My own mother was a virgin for six months after marriage because she was afraid something terrible would happen to her if she had sex. The first time I came out to her I was fourteen, hovering in the kitchen while she made fish fingers. I don't remember what I said, something about liking girls, not caring about gender, not wanting to marry a man, probably. 'Shut up,' she said, without even turning to look at me. I went into the living room and watched *The Simpsons*. She joined me there ten minutes later, with fish fingers and lettuce that she handed me on a plate. I said, 'do you remember you used to make up the storylines for *The Simpsons* when we first moved here and you could not speak the language, but you wanted to entertain me, and you made up names for them, stargirl and bagboy?'

'Yes,' she said, 'I do remember. Eat now.'

Families

In the new country, which for us was Italy, we lived together. We had arrived there escaping a war, with a job offer in hand. The 'we' changed based on circumstances, but it was always women and their daughters, immigrants from Syria and Lebanon. The houses also changed all the time, depending on the whims of landlords. There was a little girl that was raised with us for a few years in a big flat by the town square – before her parents' unemployment took them to the Gulf – who I thought of as a sister. We were the first to see her in the incubator when she was born. She hit her head on the bedpost when she tried to jump on the bed with me and my sister, something she was too little to achieve. She had very pudgy fingers and ate whatever my sister did. Her mother was much cooler than my mother. She left.

For a while, we (my mother, my sister and I) lived with another woman and her two daughters in a big block on the outskirts of the city. The one closest in age to me always wanted to read my diary. We played make-believe games with elaborate set-ups where we became separated, which made me cry. Her mother was very strict and very thin, always telling us we ate too much. Later, we lived in a two-bedroom ex-council flat in the city, with three women and their daughters: two families with one bedroom each, and one family in the kitchen/living room. My family had one of the bedrooms. We had so many gifts under a tiny Christmas tree in the corridor, all from the dollar store or Tiger, though only one family in the house was Christian and they didn't want to hang out with us, because we were not their real family nor Christians.

I liked fitting into one mattress with my whole family, sharing books and feeling wise in front of the younger girls.

In the houses the men went missing. The men went to find a job back home or in a new country. Sometimes they sent no money back ever again, sometimes they did, depending on how good a man they were. But we saw them rarely, on visits here and there.

While she made breakfast in the ex-council flat, one of the women told me, 'the Arabs are the stupidest people, because we are always coming from a war. We get a little bit of money and immediately we want to enjoy it. Look, everyone else buys houses, becomes business people, we just do our hair and go on a trip, then we live like this, in this flat with nine of us.' It was true, we enjoyed celebrating and dancing. War immigrants are different from the rest. People who migrate from countries that aren't in a permanent destruction loop want their children to have good careers, good husbands, own a house, be beautiful and fit. War parents think your house can be taken away from you at any moment. Your husband can die. Your career field could stop existing. Your beautiful body could be mutilated. Just have a good day.

So, we tried, despite the issues (mental health breakdowns, twelve-hour workdays, being paid less than minimum wage, no contracts, no husbands, no space, noise at night, someone was rude). I tried to have a good day and did not come out again after shutting up at fourteen. But then my sister did. Suddenly, I was not the only weird one in my family. I became anxious for my parents, who now had zero sources of normality. I considered focusing on dating men. I wondered if

I was the one who had made my sister gay by telling her about LGBT rights when she was younger. But I was very proud of her, and she seemed entirely unfazed by the situation. Barely thirteen, she had a girlfriend and wanted to start attending the activist meetings at the LGBT centre in the city. We started sharing gay humour and jointly turning up our noses to the heterosexual world, which thrilled me.

The other two women in the two-bed-three-women-six-daughters house told their daughters not to hang out with her. They told my mother she did not know how to raise good children. One of the mothers made a vomiting face. They said all the things my mother used to say: 'this is a sickness, and it spreads.' Eventually, they moved out, because of the fights about money, the size of the house, the cat's litter-box, the homosexuality.

Mother, take two

In my mid-twenties, I tell my mother about my girlfriend. The women have moved out a while ago and so have I. My mother tells me she doesn't know what is right and what is wrong. She tells me she grew up wild, entirely wild. With nine siblings, no money and a war. Nobody told her to do this or to do that, unless it was 'don't look at the dead bodies on the street,' and anyway she did not listen. What were they going to do?

In the war, things crumble: strict parents, accomplishments, school buildings, teachers and everything they have to say. The only thing left is a bunch of children digging holes and stealing fruit. The children have no idea how you should live your life, my mother tells me. There is nothing to live but just this very moment that is about to crumble in front of you, so enjoy what you can. So, who am I to tell you about being gay or not being gay?

Families, again

I sit with one of the women from the two-bedroom flat a few years later, nursing a cappuccino in the town square. She is the one who told her daughter to avoid my sister. She tells me, 'listen, now I have dated many men. At first, I thought the issue was my husband. I married him very young and he was very old, it was never a love story. Then I dated for love. The man I loved was a drunk and gambler. The second man I loved was nice, respectable in general, but he did not respect me. He believed the plumber over me about the disrepair in the house. Can you believe it? It would have been better if he was a drunk and a gambler. Now, I just think, I should have been a lesbian. My daughter, I don't want to see these men she finds anymore. One worse than the other, she just wants them to buy her stuff. We cannot have husbands and we cannot own houses, people like us. I tell her now, I should not have banned her from the LGBT centre, she should go, it would be better if she became a lesbian, if she can learn something from you.'

Mother, in the pronoun circle

As my sister is very young and insists on going to the LGBT centre every Monday for her activist meeting, my mother decides to come along. My mother tends to be grumpy and this meeting is no exception, but I can tell she is curious. She never attempted to stop my sister from going, confessing to me that she believed if she let her be lesbian without trouble she'd be more likely to grow out of it. I trot along for support, still less out than my sister. My mother has learned Italian now, but she still messes up the details of the language, prepositions and postpositions, little particles, pronouns. In the pronoun circle at the LGBT centre she says, when it is her turn, 'any pronouns. Anything.'

Later she tells me she does not know what a pronoun is. 'What were these people talking about?' I explain it, say some things about gender. 'Okay,' she says, 'anything.'

Families, again

At eighteen, I left Italy for Britain, escaping what seemed to me as a sunny, but fascist, peninsula for what I imagined would be a greyer but freer island. When I left these houses to make my own life, I found an endless series of queer house shares, filled with overly enthusiastic twenty-year-olds wanting to build a family out of nothing. These homes melted with all the immigrant families I'd been a part of. There were differences: the queers wanted to talk about their feelings too often; the immigrant women and their daughters never did. The immigrant women were better at keeping the house clean, but the likelihood of people fighting over chores was the same. Both had people paying one another's rent one day and never speaking again the next. Both had Christmases celebrated far away from the people you are supposed to celebrate with, but which were very fun. Both were intense, ever-changing homes for people whose blood relatives had been lost. Through war and violence. Through homophobia and violence. In any case, we were now here, ready to tether to anything, raring to build.

The thing I love in these houses is the din of family. How cousins and aunties and grandparents and friends and women and their daughters sound, the suffused ambient noise of conversations, footsteps, cooking, laughing. Waking up and going to bed to it. I look for it everywhere. The house I live in right now is big. I have a room of my own. I live with my girlfriend, my sister and my friend. There is noise but not enough. My mother comes to visit from Italy.

My girlfriend – who is English – sings Fairouz to my mother. My mother smiles and laughs.

I wonder if I am making her unhappy by not marrying a man and having a child. Not going with the man and the child to Lebanon and not doing all sorts of normal people things there. Not getting the child to play with cousins, like I used to. Nor climb on the trees, like I used to. Not getting childcare help from every aunty, like my mother used to get, not having a child who has milk siblings.

I fantasise about doing all this with the child that my girlfriend and I could make. I imagine our child speaking all of our languages, loving all of her cousins, seamlessly integrating continents, unbothered about the strangeness of our family, able to find home everywhere. I imagine the child calling the cornershop man in Beirut 'uncle' and buying crisps to share with the neighbourhood children. I imagine them getting into fights with cousins and making up over an ice cream that is half melted before they've even started eating it. I imagine them being rocked on endless aunties' knees. But then I worry about the violence. My child will never have what I had.

In any case there is a war and everyone has left. The house I was a baby in, before we left, is empty now. My uncles and aunties and cousins are in refugee centres in Brazil, working as engineers in Paris, ignoring Donald Trump in America, selling falafel in Istanbul, hiding from the war in Beirut. Those still there are getting older, like my aunty, the one who raised my mother and breastfed me when I was baby. Their own heterosexual children's children are not running around their streets all day, there is no noise of family. There is no normal to aspire to. I ran from a breaking family to another, as did my mother, as did my grandmother. There is nothing to return to. I put my hand on my girlfriend's shoulders as she sings Fairuz to my mother. There is this, now, and whatever we make of it.

Mother, coming out

My mother, who now has blue hair, comes out on my behalf to the entirety of my family. She announces, 'my daughter has a transgender girlfriend.'

I would not have told them. I don't think they like the news. I ask my mother, 'why did you tell everyone?'

'Why should I not tell them?' My mother squints at her phone and types messages to her sisters with one finger.

'Our family is terrible. Everyone has been shouting at everyone for fifty years. We are poor and communists and everyone has done something insane. Nobody cares if you like them. Nobody likes each other anyway. It doesn't matter. We just have to stick together. They'll stick.'

When I see my aunty in Beirut after my mother's coming out on my behalf, she asks me if my girlfriend is nice. I tell her she is. She looks worried. She asks me if everyone can do what they want in Europe. I say, 'I know these women who are three friends and they want to raise a baby together, they are divorced, one of them is pregnant and they are doing it together.' She pauses for a long time. Then she says, 'people don't like that here.' She looks sad. She said 'people', not 'I' or 'we'. I take consolation in that.

I want to marry my girlfriend and want my aunty to come and celebrate. This same aunty who used to breastfeed me, at my wedding. I imagine it. In my dreams there is a *zaffe* band that picks me up and walks across the streets – but which streets? – and everyone is with me, dancing and singing. All my cousins and uncles and aunties and grandparents from my tree-climbing childhood. All the women and their daughters who ever built a little family somewhere. Everyone from every queer house share that for a moment felt like a home.

I'm scared of bringing my girlfriend to visit Lebanon. I have a list of fears: street violence, damaging my family's reputation and therefore potentially their safety, my family being mean. I start discussing it with her, hoping there might be a solution. My aunty said she'd come to my gay wedding. Then, there is a war that won't stop so it doesn't matter anyway.

Families, again

My life is made up of people I love who I never see, families constantly scattering. I am always heartbroken and I am always finding. A moment in which I hold the newborn baby of my housemate and her girlfriend. A moment in which my mother's friend does my eyebrows and tells me about her childhood while dinner cooks. A moment in which I help set the altar for my friend's interfaith, queer birthday *puja*. Moments coming together in a wild sculpture of a life and I'm not sure where it's taking me, the path is foggy and I suspect painful, but the moments are all here.

My queer families are everywhere and I'm not the only one finding them. My mother found one when she was evicted. The landlady wanted to rent the house out to students at double the price, so my mother found herself homeless. She moved into my sister's girlfriend's grandmother's house.

In the house there were again three women: my mother, the girlfriend's grandmother and a lesbian lodger. It's a house full to the brim with antiques and pictures of the grandmother's descendants, including my sister's girlfriend in boxers on the beach. I sit with them one evening, as they drink wine and talk about life.

The grandmother had raised three daughters alone in the house, divorcing the moment the Pope declared divorce legal in Italy. It was a scandal. Feminism was getting big at the same time, so she got into it, shunned by the proper Catholics around her. She got into consciousness groups and owning her body. The grandmother pours out the wine and talks about the slogans. 'I wanted to destroy the system but my daughters are now all very proper, very married, they have never marched. This wine is very good, it's from Veneto,' she says.

'Drinking wine just like a family,' says my mother.

'You drink wine in your family? Isn't it against your religion?' says the lesbian.

'We drank the wine because we were cold.'

The grandmother is excited. 'So did we! Times with no heating.' The two glance at each other lovingly. The lesbian brings the conversation back to the rise and fall of feminism.

'So, are you glad you divorced him?'

The grandmother smiles 'Yes!' she said. 'I love to be alone in my own house. I like you two here, but only because you don't have to be here forever.'

'I will leave,' says the lesbian, 'once my girlfriend and I find a flat.'

'Does your mother know about her?' asks my mother.

'No,' says the lesbian.

'I know about my children,' says my mother, strangely proud.

'My children know about me,' says the grandmother.

We all drink our wine.

The future

The speechifying man in the Beirut queer house share is right. We really have nothing. It would be ridiculous to have pride. But what isn't ridiculous in a society that crumbles again and again and again in the same violence? The absurdity is what we have. Our countries are full of the holes that destruction left behind. I think of the bombed-out building I wandered into in Beirut. It was bare white concrete, surrounded by traffic on all sides, filled with holes. In one of these holes, a tiny urban forest had grown. The sun streamed into it, it was a bright green. I stopped, took pictures of it, it didn't look as radiant on my phone. Our houses have fallen. We have holes full of forest. We can grow anything in the gaps. We can have so many women and their daughters, husbands that somebody wants to kiss, men with drag queen boyfriends, me and my girl.

After the anti-gay rights gay man gave his speech, a bald lesbian answered him. She said, 'I came out to my cousins and once they got over the shock they loved it, now they feel they can tell me all their secrets.'

His boyfriend, the drag queen said, 'we should fight to have everything: electricity and peace and sexy boyfriends.'

The speechifying man went on a speech about how nobody would ever understand pronouns. Everyone laughed, everything was ridiculous.

This sense of precarity is all of ours. This constant wanting. It's not so different from the conversation I had in my aunty's house just before the queer house. It was a conversation about the revolution. My aunty, who had carried food to the fighters against the occupation when she was a teen, now carries sandwiches to the barricades that wanted to bring down the government. 'But I want my children to be doctors and engineers and live far away,' she says. 'Here, we are fighting as everything crumbles. It will never stop crumbling.' She has not been to Europe to see us crumbling there too and I don't want to tell her. I tell her that her kids are very successful. 'Yes,' she says, 'but I miss them. They are sad and lonely. We should have something better, here.' I look at the house we are in, much like the queer one: white walls, mouldy ceilings, peeling paint, revolutionary posters everywhere.

The entirety of the queer house share were down on the streets during the 2020 revolution, as were my aunties, all of them. I wonder if they ran into each other there, as they tried to remake the world. Did they maybe run into each other as the blockade turned into a queer party? As the music turned on while the soldiers neared? As everybody without a uniform became an enemy? The drag queen and my aunty both brought sandwiches down to the encampment. Did they eat them together? Was she the woman that told him he shouldn't date men because they're all a curse of the devil upon us? I see the pulsing hope that ties us together across our crumbling lives, across houses and continents. The moments of tenderness that find their way.

There is space for queerness in the Levant *because* all our normal does is break apart. Our displacement, our ramshackle lives, are opening cracks for us to fill. I continue to stumble upon families, looking for the stitch that can hold them together.

NAHID TOUBIA

MY BROWN GIRL

San Francisco, autumn 1995

It was a period of deep existential questioning. I was forty-four years old, a reluctant resident of New York City, in a precarious but steady relationship and a secure if not fully satisfying job. Perhaps it was the anniversary of my father's death, ten years before, when the intensity of his loss returned, adding to the estrangement from my siblings, the abandonment of my medical career, the physical distance from my country, that pushed me there. I was wrapped in a sense of loneliness that threatened to push me into a dark place I experienced once before. I resisted giving in to depression and with gentle deliberation, it was replaced with an equally intense feeling: a long-quietened voice urging me to have my own family. I needed to build myself a family forward and I realised I had better do it before it was too late.

I happened to be away for a business meeting in San Francisco. My partner joined me for the weekend, on what was supposed to be a luxurious pampering break. I shared my strong desire to have a child and the mood darkened. She was totally opposed to taking the responsibility for raising a child. We argued then screamed at one another, trapped in a room that was elegant and classic when we entered, but old and tired when we left. I could not stop crying on the morning flight back to New York. But I was determined not to abandon my dream to hold on to the relationship. Days later, she apologised and reconsidered.

That was how my journey to parenthood started. I contemplated my options. The first was to employ the gift of womanhood to conceive a child with donor insemination. I knew that it would be a challenge to explain the pregnancy to my family back home in Sudan and Egypt, but I would find a way. Together we sat down every evening to choose a sperm donor from long lists of possibilities: we agreed on a Lebanese Swedish Californian high-scoring student, olive-green complexion, athletic, musical. I attempted three times in a cold, indifferent clinic, but with no luck. Perhaps with some added hormones, given my age? I tried once, but I couldn't continue. I felt invaded.

I had always imagined making my family through adoption, which I now turned to. Both my mother and my favourite aunt had adopted from a church orphanage that had closed down. But how, and from where, would I adopt? Orphan girls from China were coming to the US in droves at the time. Could I give a Chinese girl what she would need to feel fully herself? I felt inadequate. Eventually, we registered for a US newborn. Social workers visited and our family was cleared. But when the call came, offering a biracial boy, I hesitated. At the adoption parenting classes they advised against political correctness: 'only go with your heart with a child who will become part of you and who you will love for the rest of your life.' The night before I made the decision, I saw in my dream a brown girl I had captured on video in the West Village. Her wild hair catching the sun, her hand clutching her father's palm, pacing the sidewalk with an assured gait. She was My Brown Girl. My heart said it wanted a daughter and I shouldn't compromise. Was I being unreasonable? Shouldn't I take what I was offered? Surely, I could love a son as much as a daughter? Time was ticking and my options were dwindling. I took a deep breath and declined the offer. Somehow, I knew this adoption was not the right one.

Not long afterwards, I was due to attend a meeting in Addis Ababa, Ethiopia, and decided to stop over in Cairo. I was going to take matters into my hands and try for a child closer to home. I reached out to my wise and well-connected elderly friend Marie Asaad. According to Islamic law, adoption was illegal in Egypt, but legal guardianship could be arranged. Marie sent me to a Christian orphanage in the Mukattam neighbourhood which was run by Coptic nuns. It was not a good fit. The children were mostly older and were from impoverished families who could legally claim them back. The next week, I travelled to my meeting for UNFPA – the United Nations Population Fund, the UN's sexual and reproductive health agency. There, I met Professor Amna Badri, a long-term friend and colleague from Ahfad University in Sudan. We chatted in the garden, avoiding the uninspiring dialogues inside. She told me that in Khartoum, babies were found abandoned on doorways, in ditches and garbage heaps. Some were eaten by dogs. The military Islamist regime of Omar Bashir, who had come to power through a coup in 1989, was arresting unmarried mothers from maternity wards and throwing them in jail. Perhaps I could save one of these babies and have my child. I decided to go back to Khartoum after eight years in self-exile. As a woman with only a Sudanese passport, there was a chance that I could be trapped in the country, unable to leave, unless I found a guardian to sign an exit permit. I decided to take the risk anyway.

Khartoum, spring 1996

My brother-in-law had died a few months earlier from an asthma attack, after inhaling fumes of grilled shrimp (a true, sad story, not a funny anecdote). My sister went from Jordan to Sudan to settle his affairs. I called her and she found out that her banker could get me an exit permit.

When I arrived in my beloved Khartoum at dawn that Monday, I found a changed country: illiberal, intolerant and visibly scared. Women were forced to cover from head to heels in neutral toned, long-sleeve shirts, ankle-length skirts and socks. At least there was no requirement to cover the face, but the morality police were whipping women for the slightest infringements of a vaguely defined code. The country was ruled by Bashir's Islamist military junta. The regime was chasing away the tolerant, pluralistic culture of the Sudanese people. In the country I knew before, children who were born out of wedlock were given a place in the family fold. Babies born in maternity wards to unwed mothers were gifted to childless families or joined others in the homes of midwives. While having sex outside marriage was frowned upon, unlike in other Arab countries, no women were arrested or killed for doing it. Before Bashir's regime came to power, an unmarried uncle thought to be homosexual was married to the *jiniya* (fairy) and loved. It was by no means a liberal society, but it was gentle and embracing of human follies.

But one thing the Islamists did not change was that adoption had been made legal in Sudan decades before.

I went around asking doctors and midwives in various hospitals and private clinics if they knew of a baby I could adopt. They all promised to keep a look out, but nothing came through. Over tea served in fine china, I spoke to the senior Italian nun at the main national maternity hospital. She told me they used to informally place babies born out of wedlock in childless families but no longer dared do that for fear of being arrested and deported.

On Friday, my sister and I ventured to the Maygoma Orphanage where we learned that the government had expelled the INGO that supported the orphanage and dismissed the Christian, mostly South Sudanese nannies. It was horrific – we found babies struggling with illness and imminent death. The toddlers were mostly boys, as girls – if they survived – were more desirable for adoption. While we were talking to the friendly manager, an officer arrived to inspect the facility. He informed us, unequivocally, that because the orphanage was a government institution, its children were all considered Muslims and could not be adopted by a non-Muslim. I was raised a Protestant Christian and the only way for me to adopt a child was to prove that the biological parents of the child were Christian. Where could I find a baby with Christian parents?

My sister had to return to Jordan on Monday morning. I dropped her at the airport and went back home empty handed. Samira, a dear friend, offered to accompany me to the Coptic church in Bahri – or Khartoum North – where the priest was known to be a bit of a rebel. We drove over the grey-blue, colonial-era metal bridge that crossed the Blue Nile to Bahri, the clean, tranquil middle class section of the three-town capital. We parked in front of Mari Gerigis, or St George's, Church. The priest met our request with a surprised frown but was otherwise unfazed. He directed us towards an Ethiopian member of his congregation who had just given birth to a baby with her Muslim boyfriend. Her eight-year-old daughter, who was living in the church, was assigned as our guide. She took us to her mother's house. We arrived in our four-wheel-drive Toyota and parked outside a shack made of corrugated metal and cardboard. The priest clearly didn't approve of the interfaith bond and wanted to entice the impoverished mother to give away her baby. But it didn't take much to realise that despite the dire poverty, it was a home of two people who loved each other dearly and who had pride in their newborn son. Muttering an excuse and an apology we gently declined the generous offer of tea. Discreetly we left a gift for the baby under the pillow, wished the family happiness and left. On the way back to the church, our guide cheekily asked, 'why don't you adopt me instead?' I struggled to answer.

Leaning against the car in front of the St George's church, I stared at the large mural of the saint stabbing the dragon with his spear. I was the dragon. It was Easter Monday and Sham Elneseem, the public holiday that ushers in spring. The church had emptied after morning mass and the streets were deserted. The world seemed to be in mourning except for the birds in the neem trees, chattering gossip and making fun of me. The cool morning breeze blowing from the Nile could not lighten my sullen mood. I had run out of options.

But my companion – who had overcome many challenges in her own life – was not ready to surrender. Samira opened the car door and jumped in. 'Let's go, I know a better way,' she said. Samira was a rebel who preferred not to comply with convention or deal with the church.

I drove the car over the open concrete Shambat Bridge crossing the conjoined Nile that flowed north towards Egypt. We passed the ancient boat makers' yard along the waterfront, before turning into the heart of the densely populated, old neighbourhoods of Omdurman with their narrow roads and alleyways. We reached a house facing a small open square, which was flanked by empty barbed wire fencing. The yard had lost its goats. The mud walls of the house were punctured by a decrepit wooden door, which was open. We went inside to find the magnificent Shadiya, her six children and her ageing mother – once an English teacher – perched proudly on her *angareeb*, a bed made of wood and woven palm reed rope. Shadiya was Samira's college friend. We were welcomed with hugs and a hot breakfast of *mulaah tagaliya*, a local dish of mince beef, onions, tomatoes and ground okra, and *aseeda*, moulded porridge made of *sorghum*, cooked on the spur of the moment. Sipping sweet tea, we sat patiently listening to how Shadiya's bastard husband – once her college sweetheart – had not only abandoned Shadiya and their children for a younger, second wife but was now skimping on sending money to support them. In the typical Sudanese generosity, Shadiya's financial challenges did not stop her from cooking us a warm breakfast every morning throughout the days of our search.

That first morning, we found a moment to take Shadyia aside and explain what we were looking for. She was excited by the prospect. A mistress of the Omdurman underworld, she flung her *toub*, a traditional nine-metre body wrap, around herself and led us out.

Shadiya took us to the house of a séance and healer. Outside the consultation room, we waited a while until two tall women finished their session. When they left, we entered the dark haze of the incense-filled room and sat on the floor, on cushions opposite the healer. There was silence for a few moments before my companions and our hostess suddenly broke into wild laughter. The healer removed the bright red scarf that was hiding her face. Apparently, she was another college friend of Samira and Shadyia and had found her calling in this lucrative business. She told us about her previous clients, who were sisters – one looking for a husband and one looking to get pregnant. She offered sweet tea, not shots from her coveted vodka bottle, which she only offered to desperate clients (alcohol was banned in Sudan in 1983 when President Numeiri enacted Sharia law). We explained our quest to the healer. She didn't have an answer but she did direct us to a senior midwife in the military hospital in Omdurman. I promised her a gift of two vodka bottles if her reference brought results.

After two hours at the military hospital waiting for the midwife to finish her shift, she finally joined us and agreed to help. She knew of a family who might be in trouble and led us to a slightly more affluent home than the mud houses we had been in before. This house had brick walls, metal beds and imported bed sheets. Through conversations with the midwife, we came to understand that the daughter of the family who owned the house was pregnant. The baby's future father, her boyfriend, was darker skinned and from a western tribe, which was considered to be of a lower status than the mother's tribe, who were from the North. Negotiators had intervened and were trying to make the mother's family accept the union for the sake of the baby but so far, had not reached a resolution. The uncertain outcome of the neighbourhood committee mediation meant the baby could become available for adoption. While drinking more sweet black tea, we learned that the pregnancy was still in the second trimester. I knew I could not wait that long in Sudan, but realising the impossibility of the situation, we couldn't just leave, either. We waited patiently until the results of the mediation were announced. Fortunately, the family agreed for the baby's parents to marry. Relieved and exhausted, I dropped Shadyia to her home, crossed the orange metal colonial bridge over the White Nile to Samira's house in the middle of the high-rise business section of downtown Khartoum, and finally returned to Villa Toubia, our family home in the modern, affluent Amarat neighbourhood south of Khartoum. In one day, I had witnessed the uniquely diverse life in the three towns that make up the triangle of the capital. I had driven over the three bridges that cross the two branches of the Nile and their confluence as they join to form the main river in a circle resembling a peace sign. But I returned alone with my thoughts to an empty, concrete three-story villa and struggled with sleep.

Tuesday, after breakfast at Shadyia's house, our now three-woman search team went on another round of visiting midwives, drinking sweet tea or orange soda and leaving the message that a Sudanese woman doctor was looking to adopt a baby. One midwife set the criteria for the desired child: a girl, light skinned, in good health and with plump cheeks. The underworld network of women providing services to other women, ranging from abortion and out-of-wedlock babies to virginity 'repairs' – whatever was needed and that society frowned upon – was alive and active. No military or religious government or their laws could ever infiltrate that underworld or abolish it. Still, no child was found that day.

On Wednesday, the team was summoned to see the senior midwife at the military hospital again. There was another potential lead. The senior midwife could not accompany us herself, but she provided another midwife as a chaperone to take us to a house where there was a baby. We drove to the edges of the city, to new, expanding neighbourhoods, predominantly inhabited by migrants and the internally displaced people of Darfur. Some lived in bare brick and some in mud houses, with no electricity or running water. There was not a single tree to shelter the car from the scorching sun.

A woman in a black *toub* was picking up squares of glistening silt from a mud pile outside a house and eating it. Nile silt is rich in iron, minerals and vitamins and those with unbalanced diets are driven to it to replace deficient nutrients. The woman was talking to a slim man who, from his demeanour and from the way he held the edge of his *jalabiya*, a loose, long attire worn by men, under his armpit, was clearly gay. Our midwife chaperone told them that we were there for the baby. We waited in the car while they ushered her inside. Soon, she came back out with a bundle of yellow and pink rags swaddling a baby. Inside the car, the experienced midwife held the baby upside down until it squealed and flailed its arms like a chicken. 'She has a strong body and good nervous system,' she noted. However, she quickly handed the bundle back over to the woman in the black *toub* when the latter told us 'we can't let you have that baby because the owner of the house is not here to give permission'. It transpired that the house was an *indaya*, a drinking house where men go to consume *marysa*, a local brew made from *sorghum*, and *araqi*, a crudely distilled alcohol made from dates.

These traditional bars, usually owned and run by women from West or South Sudan, were banned under Bashir's regime and had supposedly vanished. With her impatient, fiery temper Samira grew agitated with the failed attempt, uttered lewd curses under her breath and ordered me to drive off. Another day of almosts, mirages of hope, crashed possibilities and exhaustion. Another night of loneliness and restless sleep.

On Thursday, Samira came up with a crazy scheme. I

found it impossible to endorse, but I could not argue against her stubborn commitment. She came from a Coptic Christian family. Despite the torture her late father put her through before her first marriage, she had married again. Her second husband, like her first, was Muslim. 'I am qualified to adopt a child from the orphanage because my husband is Muslim. I will do all the paperwork, adopt a girl, take her out of the country and then hand her over to you,' she offered, sincerely. I tried to explain that I couldn't just take over a child without papers and make her mine. Still, we went along to the Ministry of Social Welfare where Samira filled out the application. She was given an appointment for a home visit by a male social worker. When the assigned social worker saw Samira, modern and uncovered, he made it clear that he expected favours of a particular nature at the future home visit. I dragged her out of the ministry building and drove a few blocks away to a quiet patch of shade by the riverside behind the University of Khartoum. I had been fairly docile, letting my two companions take the lead for the previous three days. Suddenly, I was overcome by frustrations. My repressed sun sign, Leo, took the lead.

'There is only one real thing we have found until now and that is the baby we saw yesterday. I am going back there and I am getting that baby.' Samira and Shadyia did not utter a word. I started the car and drove to Omdurman, picked up the chaperone again and headed back to that desolate neighbourhood. The gay man was standing in the doorway of a house diagonal to the *indaya* house. I stopped the car next to him and opened the window, grabbing him by the collar and drawing him towards me. 'Go tell whoever is in charge in that house that I am Dr Nahid Toubia, I have negotiated with the World Bank before and I want to take the baby I saw yesterday.' I had to show muscle. The World Bank was a supervillain, known to even those who lived on the edge of the city. It made governments remove subsidies from bread and made it expensive. The man escorted us to wait inside the house where he lived, which he shared with other contracted cooks who are hired for weddings and celebrations of pilgrims returning from Hajj. Cooking, together with nursing, was the most common employment option for gay men. We waited under the shade of a corrugated metal roof on bare metal bed frames while he scurried away to the *indaya*.

Less than ten minutes later a stout, well-dressed northern man in his forties with greying hair and plaid shirt approached with the yellow and pink bundle in his arms. He handed it to me and said, 'you can take her.' I was stunned. I held the bundle in my left arm and with my right hand quickly reached in my jeans pocket for the 200 dollars I kept there, then shoved the notes into his shirt pocket in a spontaneous gift of thanks. He said nothing, did not check what I put in his pocket, turned around and walked away. My shaky voice followed him, 'tell her mother my name is Dr Nahid Toubia, I live in America but people in Khartoum Hospital know me. Tell her I will take good care of her.' He disappeared behind the door. Everything happened in a flash. I was in a dreamlike state, not fully absorbing what just happened, overwhelmed by drunken elation mixed with deep gratitude and empathy for the mother who had to abandon her child. I had no thought of any practical consequences. As I walked towards the car, I remembered that I had film in my cheap, plastic camera. I handed Samira the bundle and took a picture of the whole group of people at the door: Shadiya, the gay man, the chaperone, the woman in the black *toub* and Samira, holding the bundle. It was the last photo in the roll and it is the only record of that moment.

When I dropped Shadiya off at her home, her kids fussed around the baby and the grandmother blessed her. Samira bought baby bottles, formula and light cotton baby gowns at the pharmacy. When we finally got home to Villa Toubia, I had a chance to look at the baby properly for the first time. She was petite, flaccidly quiet, clearly dehydrated and the stump of her umbilical cord was still attached. When I took her to the bathroom sink for a wash, I noticed she had kohl in her eyes. Someone loved her enough to paint her eyes with traditional black soot to fend off the evil eye. That moment and for days after, I sent silent messages to her mother thanking her for her gift.

That evening I felt such a deep appreciation for the support Samira had given me that I decided my daughter had to carry something from her. We chose the modern version of Samira's name, Samar, for the baby. I spent the night watching my child sleeping, making sure she was still breathing.

Friday was spent at my friend Selma's house. Selma was an experienced mother of three and took care of Samar while I finally fell into a deep, restful sleep. The next morning, I needed to run errands. With Samar well taken care of, I headed to the travel agents to arrange our flight to Cairo. The owner of the agency was a school friend of my brother. He knew I was not married, yet insisted on paying for the baby's ticket as a congratulation gift. While waiting for the tickets to be issued, the phone rang and one of the salespeople took the call. He covered the handset with his palm and announced, 'someone from the American Consulate service has just arrived in town. She will be issuing visas for two days'. The US Embassy had been closed for months as part of the sanctions against the Sudanese government. Visas had to be obtained from the consulate in Cairo. I dashed out and drove to the US Embassy. As I was being screened by the security personnel at the entrance a woman came out, looked up and squealed in surprise, 'Dr Nahid! I didn't know you were in town!' She had worked as a junior foreign office employee years before, when I was one of the embassy's doctors. I didn't recognise her, but she recognised me. I explained the situation and provided the documents, including my Green Card number, and she asked me to return the following day. The next day she handed me a letter for the border authorities to admit Samar to the US and wished me and my daughter a good life.

Returning to Egypt required an entry visa for Samar. That was granted at Cairo airport, through a phone call made to the border authorities by a senior military officer – my relative had been his son's English tutor. Unlike the cheer and generosity my baby and I received from friends and colleagues in Khartoum, we experienced a mixed reception in Cairo.

My older brother stared down at the baby with his iconic frown and asked, 'is she Muslim?'

'Babies don't have a religion,' I replied. His wife, always

warm and friendly towards me, was welcoming and took care of Samar when I had to run errands. Some colleagues found the concept of adoption strange and asked if I was not worried about unhealthy genes. 'You can't guarantee the health of the genes of your biological children,' I reminded them. Others, like Marie Asaad, celebrated us. I accepted all their reactions – I was just glad that I had my daughter.

We finally embarked on a Trans World Airlines flight to New York. The coiffed stewardesses were not too comfortable with a baby in their coveted business class. No wonder the airline went bankrupt and closed down. After a short interview at JFK airport, Samar received her Green Card. She was home. With me.

London, autumn 2006

My Mum
Nahid is my mother a saviour I should say,
She saved a little baby from very far away,
She taught me how to read and write when I was very young,
An adopted child I may be but I still have my Mum.

Samar's poem won the top award in a competition at her primary school in London. She wrote it when she was ten and submitted it as part of an assignment where she had to write about her hero. Other children wrote about celebrities and football heroes. She was known as 'the pupil with two mothers', possibly the only one. At the time, London was starting to be liberal towards families with same-sex parents. Many families brought their children to Samar's birthday parties and she was invited to her classmates' homes for play dates and parties. But several years prior, one neighbour stopped her son's playdates with us when she found out we were a same-sex family. It was hurtful and difficult to explain to our four-year-old daughter, especially as she heard him play with other children in the back garden. We eventually found out that the school headteacher (a woman) was quietly living with her same-sex partner with four biological and adopted children. They became family friends. There were other different, open-minded and marginalised families with children to connect with, some became friends, others were for the functional play dates and birthday parties that temporarily connect parents of young children.

Khartoum, spring 2014

Samar was graduating from high school and my partner and I received a joint invitation to the ceremony as her parents. We had moved back to Khartoum in 2008. Fortunately, Samar had been admitted to the excellent private school in the city, which offered an International Baccalaureate diploma. She had thrived there academically and socially. The school, owned by a liberal Sudanese family, respected the nature of our family with classical Sudanese gentility and discretion. As photos of graduates and their families were taken on the school lawn, Samar stood with pride and courage between her two mothers to mark the occasion.

Several months before her graduation, at the age of seventeen, Samar had given a talk titled 'An Adopted Child I May Be' at the TEDx SobaWomen event. She spoke in front of five hundred people. She shared her experience and expressed her pride in being an adopted child from Sudan. The audience were left in tears and there were rave reviews of her talk in the papers the next day. Her talk was courageous, heartfelt and sweet.

London, summer 2023

Civil war was raging in Sudan. Our family home in Amarat was taken by the Rapid Support Forces on the second day of the war. I was forced to stay in London permanently and took refuge in writing my memoir. But I stalled, starting and stopping, seeming to lose motivation and focus. I finally realised that the only way I could write my life's story was with honesty to myself. I had to acknowledge and honour the joy and challenges of loving women. But how will my 'coming out' affect Samar? She was twenty-seven years old with a master's degree in psychology from University College London. I went to solicit her reaction.

'Mama, I am proud of everything you are and everything you do. You should be honest to your truth.'

'But what about your Khartoum school friends, what will they say? Some of them are very religious.'

'I live in London now, I have gay friends and if my Sudanese friends will not accept you then, perhaps, they are the wrong friends for me.'

That's my beautiful strong brown girl. That's the amazing family I made for myself. The journey was not all smooth sailing, but my life would not be the same without Samar. As I contemplated writing this chapter, a caring friend alerted me to the risk of being reduced to just one dimension of who I am.

I am a mother, a sister, a daughter and an aunt; a doctor, a surgeon, a researcher and an activist; a cook, a gardener and a dancer. I am a Sudanese-Arab-African woman who loves her country and her people and who always returned home to serve them. Some may reduce me to what they were conditioned to reject, but others broke the bonds and will celebrate me. I will take my chances.

SININ NAKHLE

WHO IS IT THAT YOU LOVE?

INTERIOR. BATHROOM – DÜSSELDORF – 2025

I was already out of the shower when she tucked her hand in the wash towel and ran it under steaming hot water.

Now you're a good surveyor, Dixon
but I swear you'll make me mad
the West will kill us both
you gullible Geordie lad

Mark Knopfler's fingerpicking echoes from the speakers in the bathroom. She makes a joke about my taste in music and rests her hand on my shoulder.

'Shu hal ghanniyeh wla?! ('What kind of song is this?!')

Haifa Wehbe for New Year's Eve. Nancy Ajram for road trips. We had rules around the soundtracks we played with the rest of our Chosen Family. This song sounded nothing like us, though it takes me back to a car ride with the high school crush who introduced me to it, as we drove past the port of Beirut – back when it was just a port – towards his house in Broummana.

I wasn't sure, back then, if I liked him or wanted to be him, or both. I hadn't heard the song in ages. Strange that it would return to my feed now, in this hotel room, as I chart new waters of my own.

'*Esma* (it's called) *Sailing to Philadelphia*.'

The algorithm always knows. We giggle and the tip of her fingers trace the curve of my back. Her touch feels neither like a wash nor quite like a massage. It's somewhere in between. Like a love language, unspoken.

The smell of shampoo lavender curls through the steam and into the air like a memory. My Jeddo's garden in Hammana, the sun-warmed balcony, the way Teta preserved the perfume of crushed stems he picked up for her in small bags of cloth she tucked in the closet of sheets so they smell like magic for the *mawsam* (season).

I wonder how my grandparents would greet me today.

Coraline's phone vibrates. Probably her father. Or Ziad, our chosen brother. She silences it, straightens the towel under the sink and tucks the phone in her pocket.

'I'll call him back.'

She runs the cloth under hot water and squeezes it out. My eyes follow where my nerves can't. I watch each droplet sliding down my chest pause over the tape on my sutures before surrendering over the towel I had proudly wrapped around my waist.

Coraline's touch swishes over the grease on my skin. It lifts away the pressure of the compression vest, the ache in my muscles and the weight of the past four years. Every motion, a reassurance. Every dab a reminder that I am here, that I am held, that I am not alone.

In the mirror, I feel a channel open up.

INTERIOR. LI BEIRUT PUB – BEIRUT – 2015

The music pounds against the ceiling in LiBeirut's top floor. No one cared about the neighbours in Hamra. This wasn't Gemmayze and here, people understood – or so we thought – that Mondays were only suggestions and responsibilities could always be dealt with tomorrow, *inshallah*.

Tonight was about group hugs. Tables that could not support the weight of our dancing. Spoiled gin that may or may not drive us to the emergency room. And Coraline. Our beloved Coraline, at the heart of it all, about to leave us for Prague.

'*Bethebbo min?*' ('Who is it that you love?')

'Coraline!'

'*Bethebbo min?*'

'Coraline!'

We chanted from the pit of our lungs and over the speakers like we would at a protest, with the unruly force of years spent together stressing over university coursework, driving through mountains, swimming under cascades between them and dissecting every boring detail in *sobhiyet* gossip sessions that did not only happen in the mornings: who fucked their crush last night? How many times? In what ways? Who didn't? Why? And why not?

We archived every second in true millennial fashion, with hundreds of images tucked into Facebook albums, from which some of our family members were restricted (we were not that reckless about privacy) and, naturally, our Chosen Family WhatsApp group.

Coraline, our Coco, was the Mama of the group. The

kind of person who never missed a birthday, who had coffee with our mothers when they couldn't reach us and who knew exactly what to order before we even sat down.

I always loved – maybe even envied – how effortlessly she wore her femininity, in the most untraditional of ways that was also unmistakably her own. *Bent bladeh* (the girl from my homeland) could dance *dabke* in heels and put a VIP parking guy in his place with the raise of an eyebrow.

Always on the move, doing five things at once. The kind of person who could be driving, answering work calls and handing Ziad a napkin while he bit through a dripping sandwich.

She knew exactly how to behave at a wedding: when to kick her heels off on the dance floor, when to lean in for a three-kiss greeting and when to drop an Arabic saying I'd never heard before, like it was both poetry and the slogan of a *dekkeneh* (grocery store). The only one who could convince the bride to sneak out for a cigarette break while she handled the guests and moved the flower arrangements to where they should have been all along.

Coco always showed up for us. Late, but she always showed up. When we called, waiting hours for her in Beirut, every time, without fail, she would say, '*habibi yalla*, I'm just parking!'

Which, of course, meant she was still in Tripoli. At home, wrapped in a bath towel, swiping through Instagram reels.

But she wasn't the only one holding us together. We were all bound by something we couldn't name but knew we needed. We were figuring out the scripts we wanted to write for ourselves, not the rulebooks we inherited that never quite fit.

Together, we untangled the knots of adulthood our families never taught us to loosen, too busy asking when we'd be tying them instead. Maybe that's why so many of us hustled for scholarships and freelance gigs: to buy a little freedom from endless questions and the occasional luxury of a soft drink *and* a burger at Roadster's.

How did it feel to wear a strap-on? How do you adjust to a stepmother while still mourning your own? What do you say when an uncle asks if the girl all over your Facebook wall is your girlfriend? Do we come out at work *before* asking our managers for support? How do you handle an abusive family member without cutting ties? And how do you negotiate between faith, traditions and the desires your body longs for?

We figured things out together. And when we didn't, we soaked in the questions, together.

We picked each other up from houses and hospitals. Coraline was always the first to send the '*yalla* who's driving?' message. We cooked together, though we argued plenty – about whether to skewer the meat of the chicken horizontally or vertically for the perfect barbecue, or whether some things were meant to be private or shared with the group. We co-regulated in the back seat of cars, fell asleep side by side after late-night parties and set the breakfast table the next morning. Every time we saw each other, it always ended in laughter. The kind that bursts from the gut rather than the throat. Coco was the *aajineh* (dough) that held us together, the one who made sure no silence lasted too long. Will it be the same without her?

We swore we'd make it work. Weekly calls, yearly visits – enough to hold us through the distance. Hala said, 'when close friends leave, they become a home somewhere else and I don't mind having several homes.' But Coraline was the home we always returned to, even as we said goodbye to others along the way.

I'd watched my brother pack his bags for France years ago, stripped and dug my face in Alia's body before she left for Canada and raised a glass of arak before countless airport send-offs. We were well trained in the choreography of departure before 'see you in Beirut no matter what' became a trending diasporic mantra: the months of denial, the last-minute planning, the sudden surge of mixed emotions we medicated with mixed drinks when the final week hit and finally, this moment.

Coraline's face was buried in my chest, her shoulders shaking over farewell tears none of us could hold back. Our shirts, damp with sweat. Her own face smiling back at us through cotton: we had t-shirts with our own picture printed on them and wore them like we were part of her fan club. We loved it. Our first community.

Locked in a group hug, we rocked back and forth to the music, a pulsing mess of limbs and love. I let myself sink into it. Almost. Then, a breath too soon, I loosened my arms.

We held each other and sang, as if that could stall the countdown to her flight, as if this hug could defy the numbing rust powder induced by the meeting of geography, bureaucracy and time – forces that that were about to change everything: who we were and who we were to each other.

And yet, from the sticky floor and into the soles of our feet, there it was. The silent truth making its way to the smell of our breaths.

We all dreamt of leaving.

And we all dreaded it just the same.

INTERIOR. BEDROOM – AMSTERDAM – OCTOBER 25, 2023, 3:00 PM

'Did you notice that when you write your life story, you write like it's about someone else?'

'Excuse me?'

'You use the first person, but it's like you're on the outside looking in.'

The intern hit me with the first useful observation I'd heard from a healthcare professional in a year, but I didn't have time to process it right now.

'You're right. I … I hadn't noticed.'

Forgive my cynicism, but this is the fourth meeting she's called, not counting the before and after emotional labour and the months of waiting in between. I'm not here to spill my relationship with gender to a clinic. I just need their green light for surgery – nothing more. I'm not expecting to gain any psychological insights from gatekeepers.

But we were just getting started. There would be seventeen more meetings.

Three diagnostic surveys slicing my soul into an IKEA assembly manual no one will bother to read twice.

A bureaucratic hunt to beg for referrals from a general practitioner, a psychologist, a psychiatrist, an endocrinologist.

Visits to a gynaecologist. A dermatologist. A melting pot of -ists and experts, some of whom, to be fair, were trans themselves, just as critical of the medical complex and all trying to help.

The psychiatrist did note in her report that I was 'surprisingly well-groomed' and complimented me for being literate and aware. Of course, that had nothing to do with where I was from. Just a positive appraisal prefacing a medical opinion.

A pink and white, green light.

She didn't appreciate the layers in my answer, by meeting number eleven, when she brought up how difficult it must have been to grow up in Lebanon. Gratitude was a duty I was expected to perform.

Proof was always needed.

I didn't need proof back home. Not with hospitals. Not with the Chosens.

In Hamra, someone always sent a last-minute message and before you knew it, we ended up crammed around a table passing plates. No *afspraak* (appointment) necessary. If one of us showed up quiet, we didn't pressure them. We sometimes did the *'itab* (reproach) thing but it was always from a place of love. Otherwise, we just slid the bread across the table.

When someone disappeared, we picked up on their patterns before they realised it and knew when to give them space and when to send a '*yallaaaaa*, we miss you!' voice note. But here, without the Chosens, everything is different. Nothing is intuitive or spontaneous. No one just knows. Everything must be explained, proven, filed and approved.

I thought the hardest part of transitioning would be the internal work. The unravelling of old narratives, the learning of new ways to move through the world. Turns out it's the paperwork.

Usernames. Passwords. URLs slipping through my fingers. Consent forms stacking up. Back-and-forth emails weaving into long threads with the gender clinic, the insurance company, the hospitals. All of it written in a legal jargon I barely understand, in a language I'm still learning. All of it just to prove that my body is mine to change. The two-factor-authenticated bureaucracy eats up my headspace and leaves little room for anything else. For people. For joy.

At least I have healthcare. At least the lights stay on. At least the water runs.

I take a deep breath and my ribs strain against the binder. A reminder that even gratitude has material limits.

'Shall we start with primary school, then?'

The intern smiles, shifting her gaze between a second screen where she takes meeting notes and me, the main display. I show my teeth and glance outside, rubbing the three hairs I had grown on my chin. Still raining.

How the hell is Maha getting by in Canada? I haven't spoken to her in a while – just like I haven't spoken to Ziad or Jamil. Would they ever treat me like one of them? Would they ever let me in on 'gay culture'?

I pick my phone up and scroll through conversations. It's not rude if the intern isn't looking. I already left the Chosen Family WhatsApp group. Would it be weird to reach out now? Maybe. Probably. But less weird than leaving in the first place.

I miss them, but they've got their own lives to steer abroad.

I switch tabs to glance at the notes I'd jotted down on my phone for this session.

Please share your life story, focusing on your relationship with gender at different stages of your development.

The clinic had given me homework to prepare for this meeting. When I read the instructions, I blinked in front of the curser, thinking it would only take half an hour to submit before I could work on my article.

Then I started wondering: what tone should I adopt? Should I start in late adulthood and jump through a flashback, or just structure this in bullet points? A chain of experts, each with a magnifying glass in one hand and a checklist in the other, will scrutinise my every word. They all need to agree: I'm depressed enough to meet the criteria for gender dysphoria, but not so depressed that I might not survive the process. Depressed enough to qualify. Not depressed enough to be a liability.

They need to know I'm sure I don't want children. That I understand it's irreversible. No undo button, no taking it back.

They need to know I don't have autism. Apparently, people with autism cannot be trans. If they are, it follows a separate medical track – one that might just lead to a dead end.

This is just homework. I shouldn't care about the reader, but it's a matter of survival, isn't it?

No. That's not survival. Survival is Palestinian families in Gaza hiding in hospitals while Israel razes their homes to the ground. Survival is the little boy crying out, '*Fares! Baddi abouso! Trekni abouso!* (Fares! I want to kiss him! Let me kiss him!') Begging his lifeless brother for a kiss. That's survival. That's resistance.

Focus.

Life story. Your relationship with gender. What do you want to say?

Well, I know what they want to hear. A TED-talk leading to self-actualisation. That I'd known I was 'different' since day one, that I'd spent my life dreaming of this moment and that today, with the help of a hero with a scalpel, I can finally hop over to the other end of the binary and be the manly man I always wanted to be.

I'd heard all about this and my frustration was justified. I refuse to gaslight myself into thinking the lava bubbling up inside me is just a testosterone-induced mood swing.

Is it?

Focus. When *did* you start noticing signs?

Signs? What signs? I didn't even know what I was *meant* to be noticing – if there was even anything to notice. No 'this is my voice on T' TikTok videos. No post-op thirst traps showing off double incisions. I hadn't even heard the word 'trans' before my twenties. But – no. Wait. That's not true. I must have heard it, I'm not sure.

The first time I saw a trans woman, she wasn't even in front of me. She was in a photograph. A souvenir my aunt and her husband brought back from their honeymoon in Thailand. They were waving it around for the family in Hammana.

'*Shoufo*!' 'Look!'

They were grinning, standing next to her like she was a

circus performer, or a giraffe outside the zoo.

The photograph went from hand to hand. Everyone was laughing. It landed in mine.

My pupils dilated.

Yes.

I suddenly became slow. Handed it over and pretended not to care. Damn. What else?

Late-night television, flickering blue light. *Boys Don't Cry*. I was nine, maybe ten? I wasn't supposed to be awake. I didn't understand what I was watching. It was a rape scene. They were punishing her for being a boy(?) I couldn't look away. It burned a belief into my retina, didn't it? I don't think it ever left. What else?

Lebanese comedy skits on television. Cross-dressing disguised as a disguise. They made jokes to humiliate women. And men who dress like women. And women who look like men. Sitcoms. Gender reveal as a punchline. The audience laughing. I didn't laugh. Or maybe I did. But something felt wrong.

Okay. What about school?

I never had an 'aha' moment, I don't think. Just encounters where I couldn't name what I was feeling. I was too dissociated. Too scared. Had to push through. The changing room after PE class. The girls giggling, fixing their hair. I never knew how to do it quite like them. I wanted to. I'd press my back against the wall. Always alert, scanning everyone around, waiting to be caught. For what? I didn't know. I just felt like an imposter.

Then I wore my brother's oversized sweater in the hallway. I loved *that*. Sank in it. Felt just right.

Oh yeah, I also punched Amal. My best friend. She was also a *hassan-sabeh* (a tomboy). I was eight(?). I liked her, but I punched her in the face. Did I do that? It doesn't sound like me. Why did I do that? She said I couldn't play on the boys' team. Said I wasn't a boy.

We went to the principal's office. Madame Farouk. They brought our parents. Said hitting is wrong. They were right. But then they made us hug. And that was it.

And that first push-up bra? I *hated* it. It was white. Had *dentelle* that would bite into my skin. The underwire. It was so tight. Too tight. I wanted to rip my skin off. But I thought it was just the wool sweater. Thought it was just the heat of the house party. Thought it was –

Tariq. My boyfriend was there. Yes.

We were slow dancing. 'Sorry Seems to Be the Hardest Word.' Ugh, I still can't stand this song.

His hands on my waist. His body against mine. His erection. I pulled away. I think he pulled me back. Everything was too tight. Too warm. Too much.

All girls hate their bras, right?

All girls feel this way, right?

I looked around. Laughter, whispers, swaying bodies. It felt like the whole dance floor was in on something I didn't know. Playing a game I didn't have the rulebook for. Too tight. Too warm. Too much. I wanted out. OUT. OUT. OUT.

I'm starting to feel the same way now, remembering all this, sitting in front of my screen. Tabs open. Forms waiting. Deadlines pressing. Still raining. Still binding. Still –

Haven't written a word.

How do they expect me to write a past into a page? I'm already exhausted and this paperwork is getting under my skin harder than dysphoria ever did. I don't know it yet, but I could sure use a group hug right now.

I open Instagram and tap through Coraline's stories. A selfie with her new friends, the ones I met last year when she visited Amsterdam. They were nice. What were their names again? Gone. A blur, like most things, lately.

She'd messaged me last week. Said she's going to Lebanon in June but doesn't know for how long. Depends on the passport renewal. There's been paper shortages, delays. She asked if I'd meet her there. I haven't replied. I mean to, but –

Most days I feel like a crab that shed a shell, curled up under a rock waiting for a new one to grow. Too raw to be seen. Too visible to disappear.

And travel? The discrepancy between my face and papers, the possibility of getting stuck, my medical appointments –

I start typing. Miss you ya *3omri* (my love).

You're always on my mind (*too much?*)

Let's have a coffee call soon??

Also remind me who these people are lol (*no, wait. Where did that come from?*)

I'd better get back to her on WhatsApp before sending a DM, no? This shouldn't feel like peeling off a scab. It's just a message. But how do I choose family when I can barely sit with myself?

I stare at my words. I erase them.

And send a heart instead.

INTERIOR. AIN EL REMMANEH – BEIRUT – 1998?
Time for a dentist visit! Mom drops me off in Ain El Remmaneh and leaves for work. I like going to the dentist. I always go by myself. Dr Ghada is very nice. Her grey tools are scary, but I don't mind because I'm a big girl. Big girls go to the dentist alone.

I climb the stairs one step at a time. There's no elevator in Teta and Jeddo's building. Mom says that during the war, she and her brothers and sisters used to run down these stairs when the bombs came. I try to imagine it. But right now, there's no reason to run. I don't mind waiting at their house before my appointment. Ghada's clinic is just one floor up.

When I sit in her chair, she usually holds my head back. The metal tools hurt my teeth, but I fall asleep. It's calm there. There's no loud voices or sudden noises. Just the radio on 'Nostalgie' and her voice saying what to do next. I could stay there forever.

I reach my grandparents' door and knock. I don't remember who opened it, but it couldn't have been Teta or Jeddo. I step inside. I know this smell. It's like Teta's food and clean clothes. I don't come here as often as I want to. Mostly on Christmases and before dentist visits.

Jeddo always leaves Kopiko candy at the entrance for guests. In front of the bowl there's a table where people put their keys. There, there's a picture of Jeddo with my brother sitting on the bed in Hammana. They look serious and sad, like Jeddo's teaching my brother something important. Something only men teach boys. My aunts say this picture is from when I was born. My brother didn't like that but I don't know why. How come Jeddo doesn't have a picture of me there?

Is it because I'm not a boy?

I'm sure I took a candy, even though it's high up on the dresser. That's just what you do. Later, I probably snuck back for more – the first microdose of caffeine carving out my cavities.

I go to the living room. The television is on, but nobody's watching. That's not right. They're always here. If Teta isn't watching, she's in the kitchen cooking. She makes me so much food. More than I ever see on a table! Then she says sorry for not making enough.

Jeddo sits on the couch, like always. They fight about the television, but then they laugh. He wants the news. She wants 'Chef Antoine'. Teta always wins. One time, she made me sit on the balcony where my uncle shoots rats down the street. He wears a *flannella* (flannel shirt) and when he shoots, the rats run into the gutters. He uses a *khered'a* (shotgun with birdshot), not a *jefet* (shotgun with buckshot). That would be too dangerous and someone might get hurt. Even the rats.

On that balcony, Teta said that if Mama and Baba didn't have me, they'd still be together. That they should have stopped at my brother. I didn't really get it. Teta loves my brother more than anything in the world. Everyone knows that. He's the first boy in the family!

Jeddo just laughs. He rubs his moustache and plays with his *mahbaseh* (prayer beads).

But right now, the balcony is empty. The kitchen too. Where did they go? It's so quiet without them. The whole place feels weird.

I walk down the hallway. I hear voices. Water. I open the bathroom door and – '*ya Rabb* (*oh my God*)!'

My grandparents are standing here, NAKED!

I jump back and slam the door. I must have stood there a second too long. Long enough for the image to settle into a memory and for the memory to resurface as an image.

Jeddo was holding a *kayleh* (container) of hot water over Teta's head. Her face leaned into the curls on his chest. Sunken without her dentures, her lips are sad. Her breasts spilled over her hips, resting on the swell of her diabetic belly. Jeddo was taller, but his skin also folded into itself, like the Arabic letters he would soon try to write, swallowed up by his Alzheimer's. Teta had arthritis and calloused feet, which I used to massage with the last squeeze of a Clipp body cream tube when we were staying at their house in Hammana during the 2006 war. We gathered around the television, the news always cushioned by '*El-Helm El Aarabi*' ('The Arab Dream') playing as a commercial break. Six whole minutes to feel the grief.

Pacing back and forth, their triggers raised like arms, Mama and Teta argued over how to explain the loud noises in the sky to my crying baby cousins.

'IT'S JUST FIREWORKS! EVERYTHING IS FINE!' My mom reassured them, while Teta shook their shoulders, shouting:

'IT'S NOT FIREWORKS! IT'S THE ISRAELIS TRYING TO KILL US!'

Which made me and my brothers burst out laughing and my cousins cry louder.

Jeddo – though he, too, had to steady himself against the

sink and the grip of his nylon slippers – helped Teta shower so she wouldn't slip on the betrayal of her own feet.

It was right in front of me, on Christmases and before dentist visits, the kind of care a marriage promises a family. Hands that step in when your feet mark the end.

Does love like that have room for me?

Do I?

Back then, I turned away, embarrassed.

Today, I hold the picture still.

EXTERIOR. APARTMENT BALCONY – AMSTERDAM – 2025

'Can you hear me?'

'Yeah, but I can barely see you in the dark. Wait, are you smoking? Weren't you supposed to quit before the surgery?'

'Yeah, but it's the last one, promise.'

'Little shit! Tell me, what's up? Something wrong?'

'My mom's visa was rejected.'

'No! What?! Why?!'

'They said the reason for the trip wasn't convincing. I think that's it. Our countries are technically at war. She was supposed to help me after surgery and it got me thinking … who can I be around when I'm at my worst? Like, can't even bathe kind of worst.'

'Spit it out already!'

'Coco, honestly … you're the only one I'd feel totally comfortable with. Even if it's been a while.'

'*Habibi* … you don't even have to ask. I'll be there. I already told you, I want to be there.'

'*Hayete*, don't you have work? They've got wifi at the hotel, you can work from there –'

'Don't worry about that. I'll be there.'

'I'm lucky to have you, Coco.'

'No, *Habibi*. We're lucky to have each other.'

INTERIOR. BATHROOM – DÜSSELDORF – 2025

She runs the cloth under hot water and squeezes it out.

Her touch swishes over the grease on my skin. It lifts away the pressure of the compression vest, the ache in my muscles, and the weight of the past four years.

In the mirror, her image wavers and steadies beside mine.

Like a hand on a restless knee, I let it.

LAMIAE BOUQENTAR

TO YOU, CHILD OF OUR RESISTANCE AND OUR JOYS

Dear Sosoa,
I could start with the key dates of your conception and birth – your arrival in this world. But the truth is, we were already waiting for you, always have been. You already existed in our minds, in our universe, even in your mother's body. I'm writing you twelve hours after you were born, but my thoughts about you and feelings for you began taking form long before, in my imagination. With every fleeting glance at a baby I passed in the streets of Rabat or Montreal, with every step taken, I was picturing your existence.

Becoming-Androgynous

And yet, I'd never felt this desire before, never felt a twinge in the belly demanding the arrival of a child. No, my body didn't speak that language. Others would mention an unexpected urge in their womb, maternal desire swelling and throbbing, but mine always remained silent. I remember some women affirming, with almost visceral certainty, 'my body is ready'.

But *my* body? The phrase didn't connect at all.

I also remember too-tight clothing and fabrics that chafed my skin, shaping my figure into the contours desired by others. My clothes, which I chose myself, pinched me, as if to teach me where I was meant to start and meant to end. They kept me from wriggling away from the cutting gaze of society. Beauty demands suffering, my aunts would tell me. 'Pain is the price of beauty,' they repeated almost in unison, with a mix of resignation and pride. As if pain was the proof of attractiveness, an offering made in the hope of earning a lingering male gaze.

Put on make-up, do your hair, sit with your legs crossed. Every gesture a performance. A pact with a body that never gave in entirely. It was stretched, moulded, reduced to size until it fit into the box, that of femininity, desirability and presentability. Meanwhile, I learned to pretend. Meticulous self-control in the form of a smile.

But even as I was constrained by my clothing, by judging eyes, I felt another presence bloom. A presence deep in my bones, born of repressed movements and swallowed words. My body never demanded a child but it cried out from other labours – birthing multiple, varied versions of myself – in a resurrection of desires I had never learned to name. I encountered a body that exists not to procreate, but to deterritorialise.

And perhaps this, too, is a form of giving birth. Not to a being, but to a destiny. And not to belong, in the sense of conforming, but rather, to belong to *oneself*.

Reorientation

Though my professional field is queer research, this letter, these words, aren't academic analysis. They are addressed to you, to tell you things that I hope will serve as markers of a love that's just beginning. I remember my first encounter with the book *No Future: Queer Theory and the Death Drive* by queer theorist Lee Edelman, and his critique of LGBTQIA+ groups' desire for inclusion – in marriage and parenthood – as a way of obtaining institutional and social legitimacy. Queerness, as formulated by Edelman, exists in perpetual conflict with societal concepts of continuity and progress as incarnated by the figure of the child – the ultimate symbol of what he calls 'reproductive futurism'.

At the time, Edelman's stance of refusing inclusion within a norm resonated powerfully with me. As an Arab woman, I've always been placed inside a heteronormative framework, meaning that my life has been subjected to a series of societal expectations primarily characterised by a duty to reproduce. When I moved to Montreal, I embarked upon a process of deconstructing these gendered norms inherited from my life in Morocco. At the same time, I realised that another narrative awaited me, in the context of diaspora: the pressure of homonormativity, which, while a different mode of belonging, was just as prescriptive.

Lee Edelman's argument troubled me. It read like an attack on homonormative relationships, as well as an insistence upon queerness as a form of negativity that rejects all notions of couple normativity. And yet, shortly after my arrival in Montreal, this call to remain on the fringes, rather than seek recognition from the structures that for so long have controlled and repressed queer lives, struck a chord in me, in body and mind. Staggering under the weight of the community and the collective, as well as the financial precarity that hangs over most migrant journeys in the beginning, I had opted for the path of solitude to better find myself. In that sense, Edelman's vision offered me a seductive escape hatch – an affirmation of my refusal. Living a childfree life wasn't simply an act of personal autonomy, it was an act of defiance against heteronormativity, homonormativity and the violence inflicted by any imposed norm.

Viewing my rejection of societal norms as the ultimate act of resistance would be reductive, however. Behind the refusal, there was also fear – the fear of the burden of responsibility, the fear of failing to meet the demands of parenthood, the fear of being suffocated by the anxiety of the role of parent. And yet, during moments of meditative practice, the form of a child appeared constantly in my silent mind. Eyes shut, I would visualise myself walking through a vast field, at peace, light, a small person asleep on my shoulders.

Since my life is one of endless returns – of gendered and racialised otherness, notably – community returned to me as well, through love. The love of women, the love of your mother.

In supporting your mother in her desire to bring you into the world, I begin to glimpse the limits of Edelman's vision and its whiteness. His radical negation of the future, however revolutionary, assumes a future that is always already accessible to dominant groups. For white queer individuals, rejection remains a chosen rupture. For racialised queer and trans communities, such negativity is imposed. The future isn't something handed to us – it's neither guaranteed nor accessible – but a horizon towards which we must collectively strive to give shape. Rather than a marker of heterosexual colonisation, the future is an aspiration that can liberate us.

Amid that shift, I sought refuge in the writing of racialised queer authors who teach us that standing your ground in the face of erasure and persecution is a fundamentally decolonial act.

Queer futurism can be understood in light of the following words by Alexis Pauline Gumbs in *Revolutionary Mothering: Love on the Front Lines*: 'to answer death with utopian futurity [...] is a queer thing to do.' Loving, care-taking and building – especially when the world is trying to erase us – are radical acts of resistance.

And so I find myself thinking of parenthood not as a submission to reproductive futurism but as a beautiful form of emancipation. Watching you grow up and actively participating in raising you are ways of resisting the hetero-normative forces that refuse me that right, but also the homo-nationalist narratives that erase my racial identity while using my queerness for colonial ends. With the act of becoming a (step)mother – be it through chosen maternity or simply as your 'Moumou' – I am insisting on a future that wasn't intended for me or for the ties that bind us. With this act, I refuse erasure. I dare to dream differently. I carve out a space for a queer identity that doesn't hinge simply on negation but above all, on the creation of infinite possibilities.

I imagine that if you were to read this letter, you might interpret my candour in talking about my queerness and you as an indicator of my 'outness' in the world and my biological family. For the latter, that's not the case. I return frequently to Morocco, where I lead a life disentangled of queerness. I've grudgingly made the choice to keep my two lives – here and there – separate, just as an ocean separates these two regions. I also understand that this choice might be confusing for you, given that the world remains governed by binary frameworks: either you're entirely 'out' and therefore liberated from all constraints and have achieved complete self-acceptance; or you're in the closet and therefore oppressed and filled with crushing shame. But I'm also here to attest, through a rich existence overflowing with love, that a life of freedom is possible beyond the binary to which the world tries to confine us.

We've long been told that queer emancipation demands a form of rupture. You need to leave – or abandon – your family, just as you would discard a too-tight garment, and go elsewhere: escape in order to reinvent yourself. The dominant narratives featured in Euro-American media portray the biological family as a prison, a fortress of heteronormative values, while chosen family is portrayed and praised as the only marker of freedom. We learn, then, to view these two families in conflict, to draw a clean line between old and new, between the weight of origins and the quest for a liberated, emancipated self.

But what happens when exile, postcolonial legacies and racial violence transform the biological family into a refuge, as much an anchor as a burden? As a member of the Arab diaspora, family, mine included, is a place permeated by injunctions and morose silences. But it's also the place you go back to after navigating a hostile world. It's the place where arms open to tend the wounds caused by the violence of the outside world. The family then becomes a porous border. A territory in which tensions coexist with care practices. We learn how to move in (dis)comfort, how to negotiate our place rather than break ties and burn bridges. We redefine relationships.

In this context, queer freedom isn't a definitive leaving at all. It takes form in the cracks, in modest, minor movements, in the art of founding a family differently. It isn't simple substitution – erasing the family of origin to create a new one – but rather, hybridisation. Queer freedom draws a moving map in which blood ties, diasporic solidarities, affective transmissions and political reinventions are interwoven. Parents transform into tender and unsteady allies, silent witnesses and the guardians of stories that can't be spoken.

Liminal

'Do you have children?'
'I can't say that I don't!'

'And you are …?' the nurse asked me at admissions.

'Umm …'

'She's a special person in my life!' replied your mum.

Who am I for you? How should I be designated and referred to? How can I be contained in a single word? 'Stepmom'?

'Special aunt'? 'Your mother's partner'? I hesitate, stumbling over the syllables of a language that doesn't yet know what to call us or how to describe us.

Denominations are never neutral. They shape our private lives but not just. For they are anchored in the larger world, where they convey order and normality. Naming allows us to define and classify things and people, moving them out of the realm of the unspoken and into neat categories. The world is wary of blurred lines and fluidity. It demands that we situate ourselves within an established framework in which each role comes with a function, every relationship, a definition. It wants clean divisions and precise outlines, the better to regulate, the better to control.

But what do we do when love doesn't yield to categorisation? When it spreads beyond the imposed borders, when it is experienced differently, in the in-between spaces? If language can't contain us, then perhaps we should reinvent it. Perhaps we should refuse clarity as the only reigning value and embrace all that is indecipherable, ambiguous, undocile – in other words, 'the right to opacity', to quote Édouard Glissant, the Martinican poet whose thinking and poetry perpetually amaze me. Perhaps the ability to let live (and let oneself live) without naming, to recognise without confining, to love without assigning, is precisely where we find an ethics of love, of building love.

How might we approach the notion of 'mother' not as an identity, but as a performative act of care and as a transformation? Those who dedicate themselves the most to the work of motherhood have shown us this already –

maternity is far more than biology. It is a great relational force that shapes and supports life.

In this sense, love refuses to conform to a single definition. It flourishes in ambiguity, in flawed attempts, in the constant reinvention of human connection. Perhaps true freedom lies not in the defining of every kind of relationship, but in the ability to shift the boundaries through which we reshape the infinite possibilities of love and life, again and again. In never ceasing to imagine new ways to love and connect, to live-with, to form a family and simply, to create bonds. To that end, extracting ourselves from society's sweeping, desire-constricting narratives appears to be the path forward.

Beyond those categories that try to capture and partition the myriad forms of love and desire, I hope that you are loved – tenderly, passionately, affectionately, madly, deeply – for the more we love, the more fully we live. That same love will leave you gasping for breath, near asphyxiation, but thankfully, there's no ending without rebeginning. Lived time is a series of endless detours and returns. That same gobsmacking love will revive you; it will set your soul alight.

Queer Arab Love in Times of Turmoil

As your mother was being examined a few hours before the birth, I slowly paced through the hospital, trying to reinvigorate my mind. My stomach began to growl and, to reach the cafeteria, I had to walk through the orthopaedics, cardiology and intensive care wings. I saw stretchers pass, carefully guided by attentive hands. They were bearing bodies in struggle: withered lives hanging on by a breath, eyes heavy with pain, translucent skin bearing the weight of finitude. Before those fleeting, unsettling presences, I thought tenderly of the people who brought me into this world, my parents whose love is my greatest anchor, and of my grandmother, who is slowly fading, like a lingering sunset.

In such solemn corridors, I tried not to let the macabre mood weigh on me. I wanted to hold on to a singular light: yours. I thought of you, of your imminent arrival, of the promise embodied by every birth – new breath and unrivalled joy.

The world is both cruel and beautiful. As I write these words, I remember those of the poet Arundhati Roy, from a talk she gave titled 'The Assault on Meaning' at the Kolkata People's Film Festival in 2024: 'hope without cynicism is meaningless.'

We are leaving you, the next generation, a world in perpetual decline: the earth is drying up, forests are vanishing, sea levels are rising – all because of our indifference. Social and economic inequalities are worsening in the insatiable grip of neoliberalism, while in Palestine, a genocide continues under the averted gaze of those in power, whether they label themselves as reactionary or progressive. In Palestine, death is the only policy: lives are deemed disposable and deaths, mere statistics.

I want you to know that the summer of your birth, Pride marches across North America were rife with tension and indignation. People raised their voices to condemn the ongoing genocide in Palestine. From Toronto to Los Angeles, you couldn't miss the banners proclaiming 'No pride in genocide'. Countless attempts have been made to channel all the horror into a single date, 7 October, thereby negating all the atrocities that came before. But you should know that before that day – before 7 October – there was already an open wound, a collective memory that resists despite efforts to extinguish it.

The duty to remember isn't unique to Palestinians or to Arabs. It concerns every one of us, regardless of where we situate ourselves, as long as we carry a desire for uncompromising justice. Refusing to forget means choosing a radical compassion that refuses to recognise a hierarchy of suffering or the fragmentation of struggles.

I want you to understand the urgency and necessity of intersectional struggles, especially when the discursive machine – meaning the media and institutions – continues to compartmentalise the meaning of the term 'queer', rooting it in a single origin, a single struggle. But how can we question the link between queer pride and Palestinian liberation without betraying the very essence of queerness? If being queer means dreaming of a more just existence, a world liberated from oppressive structures, then any struggle for emancipation, any quest for dignity and reparative justice – that of the Palestinian people as much as of any people crushed by colonial violence – is and must be a queer struggle.

One day, you'll also learn that resistance isn't only about marching the streets in protest or writing manifestos, but that there are other equally powerful ways to make your voice heard. Resisting also means planting a garden in a ravaged field. It means weaving songs that will outlive you. It means learning to laugh even when danger casts a long shadow. For amid all the darkness looming over the world, there is light. There is joy. I don't mean a neoliberal conception of joy (the kind packaged in the commodifying discourse of self-improvement). Nor am I referring to some intense euphoric state. No, I'm talking about a queer joy that is critical and lucid, that refuses to look past the wrongs in the world. A relational joy that manifests as resistance to the forces that seek to destroy, erase, or deny it – namely, heterosexist forces and neo-Orientalist forces.

This joy isn't naïve. It knows the outside world; it bears the scars. And yet it celebrates what is, over and over. The joy I'm talking about is an affect – the ability to touch and be touched. It's a flame that can't be extinguished by violence. A cry of defiance against a silence growing ever heavier, a revolt of bodies against subjugation. An obstinate joy that, like grass growing over pavement, breeds serenity. This joy can be found in bursts of laughter and breaths of fresh air. It can be heard in songs that travel through walls and seen in dances that shake the bowers. By doing anything we can to protect this joy, we are fiercely refusing to be stripped of our humanity.

And so, if you don't mind, my dear, I'll say it again – this joy, fleeting though it may be, is a force. Be attentive, then, to the gentle faces that form around you, ears perked, as they listen to poems in languages the world is trying to silence. Take a mental photograph of the men and women who dance as the thunder rages, to the children who draw suns on crumbling walls. You will tame this world in your own way; as you do, remember that your joy will always be a victory.

Remember the meals you will share with those you love, the festive evenings during which music will drown out terror, the friends who will share the crushing load of the world. For while injustice can throw its weight around, joy has weapons too – magnitude and strength. Joy anchors and ensures our chance at life, despite the suffocation, despite the fear. Protect that joy. Nurture it like the earth after a storm.

Laughter, like tears, is the language of the soul. And I want to share that language with you. I want to share my soul with you. One of my moments of joy with you will be repeating your baby babbling, your coos and gurgles, which will enter my heart and take me elsewhere entirely, to a new land. They'll ring out like a melody that invites us to dream together. I can't wait to learn from you, to do things with you. I can't wait to garden together, to dig our hands into the fertile earth one late May in a show of gratitude to nature and the universe for the return of sunny days. I can't wait to introduce you to the region of my ancestors. I can't wait to bring you to my homeland, to take you swimming in the Mediterranean Sea, to walk with you across the burning sand in July. I'll take advantage of that walk to tell you about Albert Camus and the North African-Algerian sun he describes in his books. I can't wait to have you read Mahmoud Darwish's poems. Every moment of delight will be a return, every embrace a rebellion. And as long as there will be laughter to spread, dances to create and songs to sing – we will be unstoppable.

With love, Moumou.

Translated from French by Lara Vergnaud

ACKNOWLEDGEMENTS

I would not have been able to compile *This Queer Arab Family* alone. They say it takes a village to raise a child – it takes the same to publish a book. Thank you to everyone who shared the open call with loved ones, friends and through social media, and thank you to all the writers who took the time to write and submit their wonderful stories. I truly wish I had more space to include all your writing.

For the ten writers in this book: working with each of you has been an honour and I hope you are as proud as I am of your work. Your trust in me to edit your writing is not something I take for granted.

Thank you to translators Lara Vergnaud and Sophie Lewis, who helped read the submissions.

This book would not be possible without my editor at Saqi Books, Elizabeth Briggs, whose endless support and editorial insight has elevated this anthology. Thank you to Lynn Gaspard for providing a platform for queer Arab voices and thank you to Ciara Molloy, Nico Callaghan, Simon Liebesny and everyone else at Saqi for all the love you show for my book babies.

Thank you to Megan Carroll, my agent at Watson Little, for always being in my corner.

A huge thank you to my husband Aaron, for encouraging and believing in my ideas long before I even wrote the proposal for my first book, *This Arab Is Queer*, and to my family for the unconditional love that makes me feel like I have a superpower.

Special thanks to everyone who has read and spread the word on *This Arab Is Queer*, and the book clubs around the world who have selected it as their book of the month. The power of word of mouth is never to be underestimated in an increasingly online world.

I reserve the most important shout-out for my queer Arab comrades around the world. I see you and stand in solidarity with you. I hope this book provides some joy and solace as we keep the conversations going and continue the fight. We will see full queer Arab liberation in our lifetime.

BIOGRAPHIES

Abu Leila (they/them) is a writer and poet. They are currently working on their first novel, which won the Bridport Prize and the London Writers Awards. Their work preserving family histories of anti-colonial resistance was shortlisted for the 2024 Wasafiri New Writing Prize and won the Ghassan Kanafani Resistance Arts Prize. A Barbican Young Poet, their poetry has been published in *Field Notes on Survival* (Bad Betty Press, 2020), recreated as a stone carving at the Bloomsbury Festival and performed in Kolkata, India with the Queer Muslim Project. Abu Leila was born in Lebanon, grew up in Italy and now lives in London. They hope to see the fall of imperialism and capitalism in their lifetime.

Shrouk El-Attar (she/her or they/them) is an engineer, belly dancer and refugee. She is also the founder of both SEAT (Shrouk El-Attar Trust), which supports queer SWANA communities; and Shrouk El-Attar Consultancy, where she leads on designing space-grade and medical electronics. Her work has supported missions with NASA and ESA and includes award-winning innovations in FemTech. In 2018, Shrouk was awarded Young Woman of the Year in UNHCR's

Women on the Move Awards and included in the BBC 100 Women of the Year list. She was shortlisted at the Institution of Engineering and Technology Young Woman Engineer awards in 2019 and 2020. You can hear more from Shrouk on her podcast, 'El Kanaba'. Shrouk was born in Egypt but now lives between Bristol, UK and Tokyo, Japan.

Lamiae Bouqentar (she/they) is a postdoctorate researcher at the University of Toronto. Bouqentar's research considers the intricate landscapes of Arab queerness in the diaspora. Their writing focuses on bridging critical and creative practices to sketch new horizons for an Arab queer joy and intimacies as collective practices of resistance. Born in Morocco, Bouqentar moved to Montreal, where they now live, in 2012.

Karim Chedid (he/him) is a financial markets analyst who lives and works in London. Born and raised in Beirut, Lebanon, Karim has a passion for storytelling from the region. He runs the Instagram page @levantinehistories, where he collects and documents oral histories of the Levant. His historical fiction short story has been published in *seed head* (Spread The Word/ Arts Council England; 2021), an anthology of new writing from 'The Future is Back' series led by novelist Olumide Popoola. He is also co-founder of Bedayati, a charity that works to empower marginalised youth in Lebanon and was on the editorial team for its cookbook *The Olive Trail* (Bedayati/ Empower My Mama; 2024), celebrating recipes from chefs across the Levant and North Africa. Karim is currently working on his first novel.

Andrew Delatolla (he/him) is a lecturer in Middle Eastern Studies in the School of Languages, Cultures and Societies at the University of Leeds and a Visiting Research Fellow at the Middle East Centre, London School of Economics. His work focuses on race and sex in the political and economic development of the Middle East and North Africa. His works include *Civilization and the Making of the State in Lebanon and Syria* (Palgrave Macmillan, 2021) and *Queer Conflict Research: New Approaches to the Study of Political Violence* (Bristol University Press; 2024), which he co-edited. He is currently working on an AHRC-DFG funded project that traces transformations in sexual governance in post-Soviet Muslim-majority republics. Andrew was born and raised in Montreal, Canada to a Lebanese mother and Greek father and now lives in London, UK.

Alissar Gazal (she/her) works in the arts and is a producer and performer of film and theatre as well as the co-founder of Club Arak. Club Arak is an Arabic music party for the queer Arab community in Sydney, Australia and the world's longest-running dance party for queer Arabs in the diaspora. Her documentary *Lesbanese* was screened in film festivals worldwide and won best short documentary at the Toledo Film Festival in the US (2008). Alissar has recently delivered two theatre performances for Queer Stories, a national LGBTQI+ storytelling project. Her writing has been published in the *Guardian* and is contributing to a new book about multicultural theatre in Sydney during the 1990s. Alissar was born in Lebanon but emigrated to Australia with her family when she was young, where she has lived ever since. Now semi-retired, she resides on the South Coast of New South Wales where she is focusing on photography, mosaics and ceramics – though Club Arak still pulls Alissar back to Sydney to produce live music events.

Melhem Hasan (he/him) is a Lebanese writer whose debut poetry collection, *The Moon From Where We Stood*, reached #1 on Amazon in 2024. His next book, *Irreplicable Magic*, and his first work of fiction are forthcoming.

Randa Jarrar (she/he/they) is a writer, university professor, actor, filmmaker and activist. She is the author of three books: the modern coming-of-age classic *A Map of Home* (Other Press; 2008), a collection of stories, *Him, Me, Muhammad Ali* (Sarabande Books; 2016) and her recent memoir *Love Is an Ex-Country* (Catapult; 2021). Randa was born in the US to Palestinian and Egyptian immigrant parents and grew up in Kuwait and Egypt. She lives in Los Angeles with her girlfriend.

Sinin Nakhle (he/him) is a Lebanese researcher, cartoon artist and storyteller whose work lives at the intersection of bodies, platforms and protests. He is the creator of 'Beirut By Dyke', a web-comic series about trans intimacy and embodiment. Beirut By Dyke's work has been featured by the likes of CNN, as part of the documentary *Sex and Love Around the World*, and at universities including the American University of Beirut, SOAS University of London and the University of Pennsylvania, among others. His comics have appeared in *Feminist Formations*, *nY*, *Glamcut* and *Stripgids* and he has performed at Amsterdam's Read My World Festival and the International Queer & Migrant Film Festival. His MA thesis on the platformisation of queer space received third place in the LOVA Marjan Rens MA Thesis Award. He is currently a PhD candidate at the University of Amsterdam, funded by the Dutch Research Council (NWO), researching how protesting bodies in Beirut are translated into networks of refusal.

Zeid Al-Nasr (he/him) is a multidisciplinary artist working in wood, ceramics, painting and writing. Based in Toronto, Canada, he is also an adult performer and OnlyFans star. During his time as a student in South Africa, he published his journal online. He is currently writing his first book, *From Damascus to the Moon*, which weaves together prose, poetry and visual art to tell his story as a Syrian refugee and artist.

Nahid Toubia (she/her) is a Sudanese-American-British surgeon, researcher, writer and human rights activist. She is an international public health professional and a pioneering voice for sexual and reproductive health, rights and justice, centring bodily autonomy for democratic citizenship. She has served as a technical advisor to several international agencies, including the World Health Organization, the United Nations Population Fund and the World Bank. She has also advised African and Western governments on policies, programmes and legislation to stop the practice of female genital mutilation. Until the start of civil war in April 2023, she worked as founder and director of the Institute for Reproductive Health & Rights in Khartoum. She currently lives in London and works as a consultant and advisor to programmes in the SWANA region. She is working on her upcoming memoirs.

ALSO AVAILABLE FROM SAQI BOOKS

THIS ARAB IS QUEER
AN ANTHOLOGY BY LGBTQ+ ARAB WRITERS

Edited by Elias Jahshan

This ground-breaking anthology features the compelling and courageous memoirs of eighteen queer Arab writers – some internationally bestselling, others using pseudonyms. Here, we find heart-warming connections and moments of celebration alongside essays exploring the challenges of being LGBTQ+ and Arab.

From a military base in the Gulf to loving whispers caught between the bedsheets; and from touring overseas as a drag queen to a concert in Cairo where the rainbow flag was raised to a crowd of thousands, this collection celebrates the true colours of a vibrant Arab queer experience.

'A heartwarming, moving and uplifting anthology that celebrates the true colours of the vibrant Arab queer experience.'
Evening Standard

'A wonderful collection of stories, of people unshackled, of tongues untied. This surprising book allows the deliberately silenced and the preferably unheard to speak. Profoundly moving and uplifting.'
Rabih Alameddine

978 0 86356 478 9   £14.99

ALSO AVAILABLE FROM SAQI BOOKS

THE QUEER ARAB GLOSSARY
MARWAN KAABOUR

Foreword by Rabih Alameddine

When conventional language does not equip us with the tools to speak about ourselves, we create our own. Slang expresses words and feelings that break down boundaries. It is a form of protest and fills in the gaps.

The Queer Arab Glossary is the first published collection of Arabic LGBTQ+ slang. This bold guide captures the lexicon of the queer Arab community in all its differences, quirks and felicities. Featuring fascinating facts and anecdotes, it contains more than 300 terms in both English and Arabic, ranging from the humorous to the harrowing, serious to tongue-in-cheek, pejorative to endearing. Here, leading queer Arab artists, academics, activists and writers offer insightful essays situating this groundbreaking glossary in a modern social and political context.

With beautiful, witty illustrations, *The Queer Arab Glossary* is a powerful response to pervasive myths and stereotypes around sexuality and an invitation to take a journey into queerness throughout the Arab world.

'The spicy guide to queer Arab slang ...
a playfully illustrated compendium of words
from the affectionate to the derogatory.'
The Guardian

978 0 86356 092 7 £15.99